AFFIRMATIONS AND ADMONITIONS

AFFIRMATIONS
and
ADMONITIONS

Lutheran Decisions and Dialogue
with Reformed, Episcopal, and
Roman Catholic Churches

Gabriel Fackre
and
Michael Root

WILLIAM B. EERDMANS PUBLISHING COMPANY
GRAND RAPIDS, MICHIGAN / CAMBRIDGE, U.K.

© 1998 Wm. B. Eerdmans Publishing Co.
255 Jefferson Ave. S.E., Grand Rapids, Michigan 49503 /
P.O. Box 163, Cambridge CB3 9PU U.K.

Printed in the United States of America

03 02 01 00 99 98   7 6 5 4 3 2 1

Library of Congress Cataloging-in-Publication Data

Fackre, Gabriel J.
Affirmations and admonitions: Lutheran decisions and dialogue with Reformed,
Episcopal, and Roman Catholic churches / Gabriel Fackre and Michael Root.
p.   cm.
Originally presented as the 1997 Hein-Fry lecture series.
Includes bibliographical references.
ISBN 0-8028-4605-X (pbk.: alk. paper)
1. Lutheran Church — Relations.
I. Root, Michael, 1940-   . II. Title.
BX8063.7.A1F33 1998
284'.1 — dc21   98-28238
                                                      CIP

Contents

CONTENTS

Foreword

DANIEL F. MARTENSEN

The 1997 Hein-Fry Lectures presented by Professors Gabriel Fackre and Michael Root represent a distinctive contribution to current ecumenical reflection. Sponsored annually by the Evangelical Lutheran Church in America, the 1997 series was delivered, as the lectures have been in the past, at eight Lutheran theological seminaries. They also reached a much larger audience via satellite.

Their publication here is timely. American Lutheranism in these last years of the millennium is experiencing the most intense and serious ecumenical discussion in its history.

Three Reformed churches (the Presbyterian Church in the USA, the Reformed Church in America and the United Church of Christ) and the ELCA are now implementing the process of moving into full communion, based on the decisions made by the respective churches in 1997 and early 1998. Proposals for the establishment of full communion between the ELCA and the Episcopal Church, and between the ELCA and the Moravian Church in America, will be acted upon in 1999. The events of 1998 will reveal whether actions taken at the world level by the member churches of the Lutheran World Federation and the Roman Catholic Church affirm the "Joint Declaration on the Doctrine of Justification."

The reflections of Gabriel Fackre and Michael Root provide

a valuable background and a rich context for the ongoing discussion of the ecumenical advances being made or contemplated in these years. What Lutherans have to contribute to other churches, what Lutherans might learn from others, and the importance of ecumenical advances for congregations are the three foci of Dr. Fackre's presentations. Dr. Root accents the conviction that the unity of the church is not static, but is lived as part of a movement. He goes on to describe the criteria by which ecumenical proposals should be judged. Finally, he attempts to define what difference it might make if the proposals for full communion and the "Joint Declaration" are affirmed.

Implicit in all of the essays is one crucially important fact: Christian communions at the turn of the millenium are challenged to examine their self-understanding as "church" and to reconsider their understanding, definition, and practice of ministry in the church. Certainly for us Lutherans, the next few years will demonstrate our capacity, or lack thereof, to rethink the multiple ways we practice our ministry of witness and service in the world.

Preface

The essays in this book were delivered in 1997 as the annual Hein-Fry Lectures at the eight seminaries of the Evangelical Lutheran Church in America. They discuss three ecumenical proposals that were to be voted on in the summer of 1997: The Lutheran-Reformed Formula of Agreement, The Episcopal-Lutheran Concordat, and the Lutheran–Roman Catholic Joint Declaration on the Doctrine of Justification. The Formula of Agreement was intended to establish full communion between the ELCA and three Reformed churches; the Concordat was intended to establish full communion between the ELCA and the Episcopal Church. The ELCA's vote on the Joint Declaration was the first step in a worldwide process to test whether a consensus has been reached on a doctrine that has divided the churches of Western Christianity.

The essayists, Gabriel Fackre and Michael Root, belong to the United Church of Christ and the Evangelical Lutheran Church in America respectively and are clearly proponents of these proposals, although Professor Fackre's denomination was involved only in the Formula of Agreement. But their essays are not so much sales pitches as discussions of the theological and ecclesiastical issues that lie behind and come along with these proposals. These essays retain their power and relevancy long after the votes of the national denominational assemblies were taken, since how the churches receive and implement national decisions are at least as important as the votes themselves.

What was at stake in the summer of 1997 was not merely passing or rejecting ecumenical proposals, but, finally, faithfulness to the gospel and its call for unity. The Reformed Churches approved the Formula of Agreement, the Episcopal Church approved the Concordat, and the ELCA approved the Formula, approved the Joint Declaration, and came within six votes of approving the Concordat. A two-thirds vote was needed; 66.1 percent of the delegates voted yes. I trust that 100 percent of the delegates to the ELCA churchwide assembly believe they were faithful to the gospel and its call for unity.

How many steps forward are still needed?

The majority of the ELCA might argue six-tenths of one percent, or thirty-nine percent if one hopes for full consensus. Minority representatives would plead at least for some modification of the proposal on ecclesiastical succession before they would be willing to take next steps with the Episcopal Church. In the meantime, these Lutheran brothers and sisters can hang on to one another lest the step forward create a division within their own denomination.

How many steps forward are still needed?

Those who now live under the Formula of Agreement will take their next step at a service of celebration on October 4, 1998, at the Rockefeller Chapel of the University of Chicago. But beyond that service lie years of mutual conversation and admonition to implement full communion into the lived experience of Reformed and Lutheran Christians in the United States.

How many steps forward are still needed?

Lutherans and Catholics around the world will take many a vote before the Joint Declaration is approved, and it will be a trip of many thousand steps before these two churches are ready and able to declare "full communion" with one another.

From my Lutheran perspective, we took 2.661 steps forward in 1997. Nourishment and incentive for further steps await Christian readers of good will from every denomination in the pages of this book. Above all, do not hesitate to walk through the

22

Preface

Afterword by Michael Root, in which he assesses where we are now.

RALPH W. KLEIN
Dean and Christ Seminary-Seminex Professor of Old Testament
Editor of *Currents in Theology and Mission*
Lutheran School of Theology at Chicago

Gifts Given:
Solidarity and Simultaneity

GABRIEL FACKRE

An ELCA theologian of evangelical catholic persuasion has been heard to say: "We are hammering on the door of Rome so we can get in and reform it!" Beneath the whimsy, there is an interesting argument. The rationale for a will-to-union is to *teach the other something*. Robert Jenson believes Lutherans can address a deficiency in the Roman Catholic Church. He says what that is in his important work, *Unbaptized God*.[1]

Let's substitute for "union" the more modest "full communion," and more modest still, "old condemnations not applicable," and relate this pedagogical mandate to all the upcoming ELCA ecumenical decisions: Lutherans have things to teach the Roman Catholic, Episcopal, and Reformed Church-es. And it's worth asking at the same time: does the ELCA have something to *learn from* Rome, Canterbury, and Geneva?

The discussion of the decisions has circled around the question of whether there is sufficient commonality of doctrine, enough to go forward with the three proposals, the remaining differences not being "church-dividing." Commonality *is* neces-

---

1. Robert W. Jenson, *Unbaptized God: The Basic Flaw in Ecumenical Theology* (Minneapolis: Fortress Press, 1992).

1

sary for these steps. Necessary, yes — but is it sufficient? What of the mutual teaching possibilities, of mutual corrections, or perhaps even complementarity? As one of the dialogues expressed it: 1997 can be the occasion for *both* "mutual affirmation" (based on discernible commonalities) *and* "mutual admonition" (based on discernible warranted differences).[2] Could it be that the opportunities for mutual learning, possible in one or another or even all the proposals, are so compelling that a No to one or another or all of them would constitute a missed opportunity? Could "mutual affirmation" have an even deeper meaning than the acknowledgment of commonalities, having to do instead with affirming the others' gifts? Would the failure to take any or all of these steps be an act of mutual impoverishment?

Where there is vigorous discussion of the three proposals in the ELCA the focus is on the historic episcopate, or the UCC and its problems, or Rome and its magisterial claims, or. . . . While all of these are germane, I believe the questions of mutual fructification represent another entry point.

The Hein-Fry committee appears to have had something like this in mind when it posed these questions in the invitation letter to the 1997 lecturers: *What gifts and insights do each of us bring . . . ? What gifts for witness and mission . . . ? What are the theological, confessional, and pastoral concerns?*

My lectures follow these leads. Do the partners have "gifts" — charisms — to offer one another? Are the partners like Corinthian body parts that must hear the Pauline counsel: "The eye cannot say to the hand, 'I have no need of you'" (1 Cor 12:21)? And as at Corinth, identifying the gifts of each — if such there be — requires also a realistic look at the "theological, confessional, and pastoral concerns," the worries of and about each. My first two lectures will enter the discussion about the decisions by way of charisms and concerns, gifts and admonitions.

---

2. Keith F. Nickle and Timothy F. Lull, eds., *A Common Calling: The Witness of Our Reformation Churches in North America Today* (Minneapolis: Augsburg Fortress, 1993), 8, 30, 39-40, 66, and *passim*.

2

The committee asked us also to address "the impact within our congregations." The place of the congregation needs this kind of attention in ecumenical negotiations. I want to give it the importance it is due by devoting a lecture to that subject, within the framework of charisms and concerns.

The theme of mutuality in teaching and learning is actually a thread in the study documents behind the proposed partnerships. While much effort is given to making the case for sufficient commonality to view the differences as not church-dividing, a move beyond this crucial but minimalist approach is also discernible. The Lutheran–Roman Catholic and the Lutheran-Reformed dialogues especially lend themselves to this second step — of mutual teachability — because of the collisions of the sixteenth century on identifiable disputed questions, as argued in the book *The Condemnations of the Reformation: Do They Still Divide?*, the still-in-process *Joint Declaration on the Doctrine of Justification*, and the Lutheran-Reformed *A Common Calling* with its predecessor documents.[3] While Lutheran and Episcopal questions arise from separate developments rather than direct confrontations, the notes of mutual learning and even complementarity are also found in the *Concordat* and its predecessor and successor studies.[4] In passing, it is worth noting that critics of one or another proposal also focus on these themes, but do so as an occasion for *attacking* the

3. *The Condemnations of the Reformation Era: Do They Still Divide?* ed. Karl Lehmann and Wolfhart Pannenberg, trans. Margaret Kohl (Minneapolis: Augsburg Fortress, 1990), 38, 40, 52, 68-69 and *passim;* Lutheran World Federation/Pontifical Council for Promoting Christian Unity, *Joint Declaration on the Doctrine of Justification* (Working Document, English translation) (Geneva, 1996), 7-8; *A Common Calling*, 29-30, 39-40, 44-45, 49, 66.

4. See the summary observations in "Preface," *Implications of the Gospel: Lutheran-Episcopal Dialogue, Series III,* ed. William A. Norgren and William Rusch, Study Guide by Darlis J. Swan and Elizabeth Z. Turner (Minneapolis: Augsburg Fortress, 1988), 9. Focus on mutual learning appears in the essays of David S. Yeago, R. R. Reno, and George R. Sumner in *Inhabiting Unity: Theological Perspectives on the Proposed Lutheran-Episcopal Concordat,* ed. Ephraim Radner and R. R. Reno (Grand Rapids: Wm. B. Eerdmans, 1995), 206-23, 76-92, 95-110.

proposals.[5] George Lindbeck, discussing the learned and comprehensive critique by Gottfried Martens of lifting the condemnations points to this refrain, but argues Martens's failure to see the differences as "complementary concerns rather than conflicting practices and as 'salutary warnings' rather than as anathemas."[6]

While the identification of gifts and admonitions is a route into the 1997 decisions, it also has long-term "implications . . . for witness and outreach," as the ELCA title of these lectures phrases it. A more complete organism — one with all the *charisms* Christ intends for his Body — means giving fuller witness to the gospel, and in consequence, an outreach enriched by a greater wisdom of the Body, a mission rendered more faithful. Further, if I am right about the nature of the special Lutheran charism, the struggles *within* the ELCA emerge as varying interpretations of that gift. Can these internal partisanships also benefit from the counsel of "mutual affirmation and mutual admonition"?

As noted, admonition presupposes common *affirmation*

---

5. Thus: *Outmoded Condemnations?* by the Faculty of Theology, Georgia Augusta University, Göttingen, trans. Oliver K. Olsen with Franz Posset (Fort Wayne, Ind.: Luther Academy, 1992), 14-15, 22-23, and *passim* pinpoints "the hermeneutical key" of complementarity as a chief culprit in the proposal to declare the condemnations inapplicable to the present teaching of the respective churches. Missouri Synod critics of the Lutheran-Reformed proposal take the same tack, identifying the foe in just those terms in the work by The Department of Systematic Theology of Concordia Lutheran Seminary, "A Review of 'A Common Calling,'" *Concordia Theological Quarterly* 57:3 (July 1993): 191-213. A recent editorial in *Lutheran Forum* approves the lifting of the condemnations but rejects full communion with the Reformed on the same grounds as the Göttingen faculty attacked the ending of the condemnations, asserting that the case for "complementarity has been unconvincing," differences being "not a matter of complementarity but contrast" ("Ecumenical Options: A Consensus of the Editorial Board," *Lutheran Forum*, Lent, 30:1 [February 1996]: 5).

6. Lindbeck is commenting on Gottfried Martens's *Die Rechtfertigung des Sunders — Rettungshandeln Gottes oder historisches Interpretament Grundentscheidungen lutherischer Theologie und Kirche bei der Behandlung des Themas 'Rechtfertigung' im oekumenischen Kontext* (Göttingen: Vandenhoek & Ruprecht, 1992) in "Martens on the Condemnations," *Lutheran Quarterly* 10:1 (Spring 1996): 59-66. See also Gerhard Forde's "Response," ibid., 67-69.

based on necessary commonalities. I have argued in detail else-where about these shared convictions as they relate to the Lutheran-Reformed encounter, but they will emerge here in an across-the-board admonitory context.[7]

Justification: Solidarity and Simultaneity

Well, what *is* the special Lutheran charism? My answer is that of an outsider, but one in long conversation with the ELCA in one of the dialogues, in a vigorous cyberspace conversation on all three proposals preparatory to these lectures, and perhaps most of all, in struggling with my own mixed lineage that includes the Lutheran and Reformed roots of the Evangelical and Reformed Church in which I served as a pastor and teacher for twenty years, and in back of that a Syrian Orthodox and Baptist upbringing. May God "the giftie gie us to see ourselves as others see us."

To ask a Lutheran about the heart of the matter is to hear: *justification by grace through faith,* the "article by which the church stands or falls." Surely "justification" is the word Lutherans must speak to the church catholic! All constituencies of a wider Lutheranism, and all the intra-ELCA partisans, return ever and again to it. Yet, a case could be made that the doctrine of justification is central for others in the Reformation family, often described as its "material principle," the authority of Scripture being the "formal principle." So *Invitation to Action,* a joint North American Lutheran-Reformed document:

7. I have argued the case for "commonality" as well as mutual corrigibility elsewhere. See "Summary Observations" in *The Leuenberg Agreement and Lutheran-Reformed Relationships: Evaluations by North American and European Theologians,* ed. William G. Rusch and Daniel Martensen (Minneapolis: Augsburg, 1988), 125-32; "Mutual Conversation, Consolation and Correction," *Dialog* 29: 2 (Spring 1990): 88-91; "What Lessons Does the Consultation Suggest for the Future Work of the E.L.C.A.?" *Journal of Ecumenical Studies* 28:3 (Summer 1991): 472-74; "Call and Catholicity," *Pro Ecclesia* 1:1 (Fall 1992): 20-26; "Response to Chapman," *Lutheran Forum* 27:3 (August 1993): 18-19; "Pleading the UCC Case," *Forum Letter* 25:9 (September 1996): 6-8; "The ELCA and the UCC," *Dialog* 36:2 (Spring 1997): 147-49.

Both Lutheran and Reformed traditions confess this gospel in the language of justification by grace through faith alone. This doctrine of justification was the central theological rediscovery of the Reformation; it was proclaimed by Martin Luther and John Calvin and their respective followers.[8]

And "evangelicalism," as the word is used widely today, claims the same defining characteristic, albeit as radically subjectivized in a "born again" experience.[9]

While there may be this wider affirmation of the centrality of justification, I shall argue that justification is still the special gift brought by Lutherans to the church catholic, but justification understood in a *special Lutheran way*. The particularity of this charism has to do with Lutheran convictions about *how* justification comes to us.

Over time in Lutheran theology, piety, and practice, two "how" refrains appear: (1) justifying grace comes where promised as *haveable* (the word is Bonhoeffer's), a "condescension Christology" expressed in the assured continuing divine *solidarity* with us; and (2) the alien righteousness so conferred is upon those who are *simultaneously* sinners and justified.

In historic struggles between Lutherans and others, these emphases of "solidarity" and "simultaneity" came to be formulated in familiar Latin watchwords: *finitum capax infiniti*, the finite as capable of [bearing] the Infinite; and *simul iustus et peccator*, at

---

8. "Joint Statement on Justification," *Invitation to Action: The Lutheran-Reformed Dialogue, Series III, 1981-1983*, ed. James E. Andrews and Joseph A. Burgess (Philadelphia: Fortress, 1984), 9.

9. See the writer's entry, "Evangelical, Evangelicalism," *Dictionary of Christian Theology* (Philadelphia: Westminster Press; London: SCM Press, 1983), 191-92.

Recent Reformation–Roman Catholic dialogues might even suggest that the Roman Catholic tradition can be added to those who, in some sense, give pride of place to justification, willing to say that "the doctrine of justification always retains a special function . . . as the touchstone for testing at all times whether its proclamation and its praxis correspond to what has been given to it by its Lord." *The Condemnations of the Reformation Era: Do They Still Divide?*, 69.

the same time righteous and sinner. These "motifs" of *haveability* and *simultaneity* — justification cum *capax* and *simul* — are a Lutheran gift to the church catholic and a needed word to be heard by the ELCA's proposed ecumenical partners. The *capax*, having less current visibility in Lutheran self-definition than the *simul*, will receive more attention.

Divine Solidarity

In *Act and Being*, Dietrich Bonhoeffer says:

> God *is there*, which is to say: not in eternal non-objectivity . . . [but] "haveable," graspable in his Word within the church.[10]

Bonhoeffer is challenging the early Barth, making use of the Lutheran christological *capax* teaching. As Bethge describes it:

> Bonhoeffer suspects here [in Barth] the old Extra-Calvinisticum which does not allow the glory of God to enter entirely into this world. *Finitum incapax infiniti*, the Calvinists say. Bonhoeffer protests with Luther against this all his life. *Finitum capax infiniti*. . . .[11]

Stated or presupposed here are the familiar Lutheran refrains of: (1) the rejection of the Calvinist "beyond" — *extra Calvinisticum* (the teaching that after the Incarnation, the eternal Son was not restricted to the flesh); (2) the interchangeability of the

---

10. Dietrich Bonhoeffer, *Act and Being*, trans. Bernard Noble (New York: Harper and Bros., 1961), 90-91.

11. Eberhard Bethge, "Bonhoeffer's Life and Theology," in *World Come of Age*, ed. Ronald Gregor Smith (Philadelphia: Fortress Press, 1967), 36-37. At the same time, Bonhoeffer's friendship with, and debt to, Karl Barth cannot be overstated. The recent discovery of some early Bonhoeffer letters gives added corroboration of the latter. See Wallace Alston and Michael Welker, "Dietrich Bonhoeffer: Previously Unpublished Letters to Paul Lehmann," *Theology Today* 53:3 (October 1996): 289-98.

properties of the divine and human natures of Christ *(communicatio idiomatum);* (3) the finite as capable of the Infinite. While these are christological themes, they often appear in sixteenth-century Lutheran-Reformed debates on the eucharist. My contention will be that the last formulation, *finitum capax infiniti,* is not an intrusive or irrelevant "philosophical principle" but a way of expressing the special Lutheran understanding of how justification comes *now* to us.[12] Thus in *Act and Being* Bonhoeffer traces the line from Lutheran condescension Christology into the church and its sacraments, citing the earthy language of Luther:

> It is the honour and glory of our God . . . that, giving himself for our sake in deepest condescension, he passes into the flesh, the bread, our hearts, our mouths, entrails, and suffers also for our sake that he be dishonourably *(unehrlich)* handled, on the altar as on the Cross.[13]

Remember the "thereness" of the God who risks Presence among us, the bloody God of the cross and altar, the God who has, in Bethge's words,

> bound himself socially in vicarious acting . . . the historical faithfulness of God [that] includes temporality, historicity, involvement. . . .[14]

Be wary of mesmerisms with the divine sovereignty, ones that distance God from the finitudes of time and space! Don't let the

12. As in the otherwise excellent study of the "extra Calvinisticum" by David Willis-Watkins, who too quickly dismisses it as a "philosophical principle" while at the same time exploring the importance of the divine sovereignty in Calvin's thought to which the *non capax* points. See David Watkins, *Calvin's Catholic Christology: The Function of the So-Called Extra Calvinisticum in Calvin's Theology* (Leiden: E. J. Brill, 1966), 2-4.

13. Martin Luther, WA 23.157, quoted by Dietrich Bonhoeffer, *Act and Being,* 81.

14. Bethge, *World Come of Age,* 37, 38.

focus on the majesty of God obscure the humiliation of God in Christ and all his benefits.

The *capax* so understood is God *with us* in church, sacraments, proclamation, present in things tangible, tasteable, audible. Christ, the Son of the Father, is in solidarity with us, unambiguously available by his grace and choice — not brought by, nor kept from us, by our works — but by the promise of the one trustworthy Promise-Keeper. Hence the importance of the "is" — "this *is* my body" — that gives assurance to the terrified conscience. If in the sixteenth century "the major function of justification by faith was . . . to console anxious consciences terrified by the inability to do enough to earn or merit salvation,"[15] then the availability of God in finite media is crucial. This saving grace *for me*, personally, is also corporate, *for us*. Whatever else the *satis est* of AC7 means, it gives the firm assurance that in these accessible, rightly used means of grace — Word and sacrament — the saving promises of God are unfailingly kept.

The Lutheran-Reformed document, *A Common Calling*, basic to the current proposal for Lutheran-Reformed full communion, shows how divine solidarity comes to the fore in what it calls Lutheran eucharistic "emphases." They all circle about the "have-able": the assertion of (1) "the bodily presence of the complete Christ" and thus the rejection of "the dissolution of the presence into a merely internal reality brought about by a subjective act of faith . . . memorialism"; (2) "the link between the Lord's true body and the elements, saying that the Lord is present, given and received 'in, with and under' bread and wine" and with it the rejection of the sacrament as "spiritual symbolism"; (3) "that even unbelievers or unworthy recipients eat and drink the true body and blood of Christ *(manducatio impiorum)*" and with it the rejection of "the dissolution of Christ's objective presence into a subjective construction";

15. "History of the Question," *Justification by Faith (Common Statement)*, *Justification by Faith: Lutherans and Catholics in Dialogue*, VII, ed. H. George Anderson, T. Austin Murphy, and Joseph A. Burgess (Minneapolis: Augsburg, 1985), 23.

(4) the "interchange of properties *(communicatio idiomatum)*" assuring "the presence of the divine and human in the Lord's Supper" and the rejection of "a Nestorian division of the one Christ into two, of whom only the divine person is present in the Supper"; (5) the assertion of the "ubiquity of Christ's human and divine natures after the resurrection and ascension . . . to explain the simultaneity of the Lord's bodily presence in many places at one and the same time" and with it the rejection of "a local circumscription."[16]

My contention is that in these eucharistic formulas, with their christological backdrop, and wider import in the *finitum capax infiniti*, a Lutheran witness is made to the divine *solidarity* with a fallen world through its finite mediums, not only vis-à-vis the Reformed tradition, but to the church catholic. For Lutherans, as Martin Heinecken asserts: "The central issue is . . . that the finite is capable of the infinite."[17]

Lutheran Admonitions

Several American church historians — Winthrop Hudson, a Baptist, and Mark Noll, a Presbyterian — have both noted the importance of what Noll calls "the Lutheran difference." Noll sees it as a challenge to the pervasive anthropocentrism and works-righteousness of both his own evangelical constituency and of mainline religion in America. He says Lutherans never let us forget

> that *God* saves in baptism, that *God* gives himself in the Supper, that *God* announces his Word through the sermon, that *God* is the best interpreter of his written Word — these Lutheran con-

16. Quotations are from *A Common Calling*, 46-47.

17. Martin J. Heinecken, "Christology, The Lord's Supper and its Observance in the Church," *Marburg Revisited: A Reexamination of Lutheran and Reformed Traditions,* ed. Paul C. Empie and James I. McCord (Minneapolis: Augsburg Publishing House, 1966), 90.

victions are all but lost in the face of American confidence in human capacity.[18]

Here is the divine solidarity, the *capax*, God's promise kept to be *with us*.

Interestingly, the various areas Noll mentions correspond to constituencies within Lutheranism that gravitate toward one or another mode of haveability: sacraments celebrated, Word proclaimed, Word written. I shall return to these internal Lutheran divisions. Yet, Noll's overall point is telling: non-Lutherans need to be admonished about the divine solidarity "in, with and under" ecclesial *givens*.

Striking a similar note, Methodist pastor Paul Stallworth declares that we must look to Lutherans for "fire in the belly" to resist cultural seductions.[19] If the Triune God is inseparable from "the givens" — life together in Word, sacrament, creed, and confession — then "hands off" this Body of Christ, you ideologues![20] Episcopal defenders of the Concordat strike the same note, citing the importance of the Lutheran stress on doctrinal integrity.[21] In fact a case can be made that it has been the Lutheran concern for

18. Mark Noll, "The Lutheran Difference," *First Things*, Issue 2 (February 1992): 39. Earlier Hudson had written in the same vein, speaking of the Lutheran emphasis on the relationship of grace to "a confessional tradition, a surviving liturgical structure, and a sense of community, which, however much it may be the product of cultural factors, may make it easier for them than most Protestant denominations to recover 'the integrity of church membership' without which Protestants are ill-equipped to participate effectively in the dialogue of a pluralist society." Winthrop S. Hudson, *American Protestantism* (Chicago: University of Chicago Press, 1961), 176, quoted in Carl Braaten, *Justification: The Article by Which the Church Stands or Falls* (Minneapolis: Fortress Press, 1990), 2.

19. Paul T. Stallsworth, "Time of Crisis, Time to Confess," *Lutheran Forum* 27:3 (August 1993): 50-53.

20. Nicely illustrated in South Africa and Namibia, where, according to one observer, the Lutheran Churches refused to allow ideology to compromise their witness and challenged the status quo. Letter from Christopher Niebuhr, July 14, 1996.

21. As in the comments of R. R. Reno in "The Evangelical Significance of the Historic Episcopate," *Inhabiting Unity*, 91.

the haveable sedimentations of *doctrine* that accounts for the high level of theological concern and conversation in all the bilateral discussions in which they have been involved, with that influence spilling well beyond its own ecumenical agenda.

The importance of the testimony to the divine solidarity, of course, comes crystal clear in the eucharistic controversies, and specifically the legitimate critique of Zwinglianism. No haveable Presence in this memorialism! The assurance of justification itself is compromised if we cannot believe Christ's own word: "This *is* my body."[22] The finite bread *is* capable of receiving the Infinite, and the promise of Christ kept. It should be noted, as John Williamson Nevin details in *The Mystical Presence*,[23] that the doctrine of the Supper found in Calvin and in the Reformed Confessions consistently asserts that Presence, although one in which the Holy Spirit enters to bring the glorified humanity of Christ to the communicant, reflecting thereby the stress on the divine *sovereignty* in the Reformed tradition, rightful companion to the divine *solidarity*, a subject to be explored in my second lecture. But here we underscore how crucial the Lutheran charism is as an integral part of the body of Christian teaching and practice.

Lutheran admonitions are especially in order in the present dialogues. To the Reformed partners the question must be put: Has your implacable stress on the divine sovereignty led you to the determinisms of predestination, on the one hand, or universalism, on the other? Have you so focused on the divine majesty in your understanding of the church, the sacraments, and Scripture that the promise of the holy God to be among us has been denied and these arenas left to the devices of good works? Has your featuring of imperatives instead of indicatives (your "always reforming" slogan) sacrificed the perennial truth of the

22. So, for example, Luther's indictment of the "fanatics" in "The Sacrament of the Body and Blood of Christ — Against the Fanatics," and "Confession Concerning Christ's Supper" in *Martin Luther's Basic Writings*, ed. Timothy F. Lull (Minneapolis: Fortress Press, 1989), 314-40, 375-404.

23. John Williamson Nevin, *The Mystical Presence and Other Writings on the Eucharist*, Lancaster Series on the Mercersburg Theology, vol. 4, ed. Bard Thompson and George Bricker (Philadelphia: United Church Press, 1966).

ecumenical creeds and Reformation confessions to the quest for change and novelty?

To the Episcopal/Anglican partner some of the same questions must be put, together with: Has your trust in the historic episcopacy to secure the apostolicity of the church, and your relegation of the Articles of Religion in *The Book of Common Prayer* to the status of "Historical Documents of the Church," not diminished the importance of apostolic faith, as might be argued by the departure from it of some in the very historic episcopacy that is presumed to guarantee apostolic faith? (The 1996 revisions of the Concordat that add the specifics of doctrinal agreement reflect that concern, and thus testify to the needed mutual admonition.)[24]

And to the Roman Catholic partner these questions must be put: Has the defining revelatory "haveability" in Scripture been compromised by the ever-new development of doctrine under the aegis of a privileged magisterium? And related to that, what of the current unclarities in the *Joint Declaration on Justification* on the status of justification by faith as either *"the,"* or only *"a,"* criterion that "orients all teaching and practices"? (The latter is the present wording, while earlier Lutheran–Roman Catholic documents spoke of *"the."*)[25]

An Intra-Lutheran Excursus

The Lutheran witness to the *thereness* of God takes different forms. Current differences within the ELCA can be traced to varying views on justification that align with this motif, including the

24. For the revision see "Agreement in the Doctrine of the Faith," in "Official Text," *Concordat of Agreement, Lutheran-Episcopal and Lutheran-Reformed Ecumenical Proposals* (Chicago: Office of the Bishop, Evangelical Lutheran Church in America, 1996), 7-8. Other discussion of this matter includes O. C. Edwards, "The Concordat of Agreement and a Common Calling in the Context of Faith and Order and COCU," *Ecumenical Trends* 23:8 (September 1994): 1.

25. See the discussion of this by Joseph H. Burgess, "On Lifting the Condemnations," *Dialog* 36:1 (Winter 1997): 64-65.

ecumenical preferences of one or another constituency.[26] A much-commented-upon division within the ELCA, of course, is between "evangelical catholic" and "confessional" Lutherans. While historical, sociological, and geographical factors enter the picture, differences here can also be interpreted as variations on justification-cum-*capax,* a disagreement based on *where* the promise of justification is kept: in tangible conduits, sacramental and magisterial, or in confessional givens? In visibilities or audibilities? Or in the context of debates about the apostolicity of the church, does the latter depend on apostolic ministry or apostolic doctrine?[27]

Episcopal observer R. Reno recently tracked these intra-ELCA differences (with his own 1997 agenda), juxtaposing an evangelical catholic *capax* (relying on Robert Jenson and Eric Gritsch's interpretations in *Lutheranism*) to what he calls the "radical and dialectical view" represented by Gerhard Forde. Concerned that the latter devolves into "dialectical explosions," Reno holds instead that

> the unconditional promise of justification creates and presupposes important conditions which are entailed by the very logic of God's unconditional love. . . . The gospel promise is not a dialectical instance of self-destructing mediation. Instead the evangelical catholic view affirms a real presence which simply *is* divine. . . . Justification involves a rebirth made possible by a *permanent* and *triumphant* divine presence on *this* side of the divide.[28]

26. As discussed for example by Carl Braaten in *Justification: The Article by Which the Church Stands Or Falls* (Minneapolis: Fortress Press, 1990), 10-18.

27. While in principle tending toward one or the other partner in full communion, evangelical catholics can have their reservations about the Concordat and confessional Lutherans about the doctrinal seriousness of the Reformed. On the former see Leonard Klein's evangelical catholic lament about the Episcopal Church in "Justification and Moral Authority," *Lutheran Forum* 30:3 (September 1996): 6-7. On the latter, see G. G., "Reformed and Episcopal Ecumenics: Death and Sickness Unto Death," *Dialog* 36:1 (Winter 1997): 5.

28. R. R. Reno, "The Doctrine of Justification: Lutheran Lessons for Anglicans in Search of Confessional Integrity," *Pro Ecclesia* 3:4 (Fall 1994): 469-70, 471-72.

Justification, so understood, comes to us "in carnal form," which means:

> The evangelical and catholic theologian must be open, in principle, to the possibility that the historic episcopate might be the soteriological condition of the gospel.[29]

Reno rightly perceives the function of the *capax* — the haveability of justification through "ontological presence . . . temporal location . . . carnal form" — in its evangelical catholic expression. And he rightly distinguishes it from another Lutheran interpretation of the *how* of justification. However, Reno's dismissive treatment of "dialectical explosions" fails to recognize that Forde's view is a Lutheran variation on the divine solidarity associated in his case with the audibilities rather than the tangibilities, the "Word proclaimed" rather than the episcopacy continued.

Yet a twofold typology does not exhaust Lutheran variations on the motif of *capax*. Lutheran pietism locates the continuing and justifying divine solidarity with us in the believing heart: God is "there" in the *experience* of the forgiven sinner, the "blessed assurance," the happening of grace *pro me*.[30] In yet other theo-

---

29. Reno, 474.

30. In "evangelical" Lutheranism, justification is inseparable from the personal knowledge of being all known and all forgiven. Both sacramental fidelity and doctrinal purity are necessary, but not sufficient. The final ramparts of the fortress are in the heart, not on the altar or in the catechism: "you must be born again."

But there are open gates in this fortress that make for a pietist ecumenical agenda, too open for the "catholic" and the "confessionalist." The spyglass of these critics spot lowered drawbridges: a desire too quickly to find a commonality in the heart with others who are sacramentally or doctrinally suspect. The often-cited showcase in North America of this presumed indifferentism is "Smuckerism," and in Europe the Prussian Church preacher, Schleiermacher, the "Moravian of a higher order" in whom unionism and pietism joined to dissolve the disciplines of doctrine and governance.

While "existentialism" is worlds away from pietism, both make the move to interiority. What is true must be true *for me*. Søren Kierkegaard's struggle against "the crowd," including the "Christian crowd," and the self-

logical constituencies within a wider Lutheranism, the inerrancy of Scripture's autographs is the locus of the *capax*. And further, can the vocal social activist constituency in the ELCA be understood as very much in the late Bonhoeffer tradition? Here the "haveability" of the suffering God is through participation in the sufferings of God in the sufferers of this world, the outworking in Bonhoeffer's theology of the *capax*, argued convincingly by James Burtness some years ago.[31]

---

forgetfulness of the speculative thinker has clear continuities with deeply self-involving Lutheran piety. Lutheran Bishop Grundvig, for whom the "haveability" of Christ was inextricable from the church and its objectivities, was a predictable target for Kierkegaard, reflecting the different location of the *capax* in varied Lutheran traditions. On Kierkegaard's assault on the "objectivities" in both church and culture see the writer's "The Concept of Alienation in the Thought of Kierkegaard and Marx," University of Chicago Ph.D. dissertation, 1962.

31. James Woeffel asserts the linkage between the Lutheran *capax* and Bonhoeffer's later theology of the secular: "Here is the key to Bonhoeffer's whole theological method, *including the final 'non-religious interpretation of religious concepts.'* " James W. Woeffel, *Bonhoeffer's Theology: Classical and Revolutionary* (Nashville: Abingdon Press, 1970), 141.

James Burtness in an important essay on the relation of Barth to Bonhoeffer follows the train of the Lutheran condescension Christology in Bonhoeffer from *Act and Being* through *The Communion of Saints* and *Life Together* to *Ethics* and *Letters and Papers from Prison* (James H. Burtness, "As Though God Were Not Given: Barth, Bonhoeffer, and the *Finitum Capax Infiniti*," *Dialog* 19 (Fall 1980): 249-55. I am in debt to John Godsey, Barth and Bonhoeffer scholar, for his thoughts on this subject and for directing me to this important article. Richard Bliese, who has done significant work on Bonhoeffer, has also been of help in showing me the Lutheran cast of Bonhoeffer's thought. Burtness argues that the "new standpoint" for interpreting the Lutheran tradition, mentioned as such by Bonhoeffer in *Act and Being*, moved to a point of view in *Ethics* that "*embraces the capax* totally and unreservedly and recklessly expands its use from Christology and the Lord's Supper to a vast vision of God" (Burtness, 252). The *Letters* carry this interpretation further, as on May 5, 1944: "What is above the world is, in the Gospel, intended to exist for the world — I mean that not in the anthropocentric sense of liberal, mystic, pietistic, ethical theology, but in the biblical sense of creation, and of the incarnation, the crucifixion and resurrection of Jesus Christ." Dietrich Bonhoeffer, *Letters and Papers from Prison*, Greatly Enlarged Edition, ed. Eberhard Bethge (New York: Macmillan, 1971), 286. Burtness comments: "If the finite is, because of God's condescension in Jesus Christ

If this is a correct reading of Lutheran variations on justification, it has implications for the controversies within the ELCA today. Is it a plea for intra-Lutheran ecumenicity, an occasion within its ranks for both "mutual affirmation" and "mutual admonition"?

Simultaneity

Justification in Lutheran interpretation is inseparable from the motif of *simul iustus et peccator*. While the haveability of Christ is assured *in* one or other of the means cited, God's resolute grace comes to us *as* receiving sinners. Our continuing rebellion cannot turn aside the unconditional "in-spite-of" Agape. Justification is by God's grace to sinners, not by the good works of purported saints. The struggle with sin *persists* in the life of the redeemed. The insistence on the simultaneity of sin and justification is a measure of the profound Lutheran realism about the human condition. However acknowledged, as a new heart . . . pre-disposition . . . orientation, Lutherans have no illusions about the depth of the fall and its continuing effects in the journey of the believer.

Astringent realism about the human condition expresses itself not only in this area of subjective soteriology, but also in the Lutheran distinction in the public sphere between law and Gospel, in its view of the orders of preservation, "the left hand of God," and the masks of God. In all these cases, the continuing state of the fall so asserts itself that it must be

---

. . . that . . . is the kind of talk that drives one to Christ (and thus to God and the world)" (Burtness, 254).

If the finite *world*, like the bread and wine, is capable of bearing the incarnate Christ, then there in *its* own mode, as in the eucharist and its own mode, we are called to "participate in the sufferings of God." Those who put high on the Lutheran mission agenda the call to worldly witness and solidarity with the sufferer, whether explicitly or not, keep company with Bonhoeffer in appropriating and reinterpreting the Lutheran *capax* tradition.

exposed by the law and restrained by the divine orderings and actions.

How important this charism is for Christians innocent of the ambiguities of the Christian life! Or for any painter on the larger canvas of human life who knows nothing of chiarascuro! The Lutheran eye sees the night that attends the light. All assumptions of untrammeled advance, whether the perfectionisms of the pious or the utopianisms of the political, need the Lutheran caveat. Simple juxtaposition of saints and sinners, again whether pious or political, requires the Lutheran witness to the persistence of sin in the presumed righteous and therefore the rejection of the manichaean "us and them" of sectarian Christianity and the secular ideologies of the right or left, not infrequently in alliance in the Religious Right and Religious Left.[32]

This gift/admonition is needed by all three of the dialogue partners where: (1) the accent on *sanctification* in the Reformed, Roman Catholic, and Anglican traditions encourages elitist illusions about the spiritual life, a too-simple distinction between saints and sinners or theologies with Pelagian or semi-Pelagian drift; (2) the accent on sanctification invites illusory hopes for personal or social history; (3) emphases on "works of love," "merit," and talk of the cooperation of a free will in the processes of salvation lead easily and historically to "works-righteousness"; (4) the accent on the inseparability of church order from Christian faith in the Reformed, Roman Catholic, and Anglican (whether it be congregational, presbyteral, or episcopal) traditions obscures the ambiguity of ecclesial institutions. In all cases, the Lutheran eye sees better than most the temptation to fuse too quickly the Not Yet with the Now, to take possession of what is only given out of divine mercy. And in matters of public history, the law/gospel distinction, the differentiation between orders of creation and redemption, the wariness of the church *qua* church engaging the political powers

32. So the argument of the author's *Religious Right and Christian Faith* (Grand Rapids: Wm. B. Eerdmans, 1983).

and principalities with the vocation of the Christian *within* those structures as alternative, are variations on the Lutheran realism about the persistence of sin in human life.[33]

There may well be another Lutheran deployment of the *simul*, in matters epistemological as well as soteriological. So Pannenberg's assertion:

> Dogmatics may not presuppose the divine truth which the Christian doctrinal tradition claims. Theology . . . must treat it as an open question and not decide it in advance. . . . Even the question of God's reality, of his existence in view of his debateability in the world as atheistic criticism in particular articulates it, can find a final answer only in the event of eschatological world renewal. . . .[34]

— or Ronald Thiemann's comparable declaration about the modesty appropriate to revelatory claims of "knowledge":

> The justifiability of one's faith and hope in the trustworthiness of a promiser is never fully confirmed (or disconfirmed) until the promiser actually fulfills (or fails to fulfill) his/her promises. Until the moment of fulfillment the recipient must justify faith and hope on the basis of a judgment concerning the character of the promiser . . . consequently we live in a situation in which there can be no indubitable foundation for knowledge and thus in which both belief and refusal to believe can appear to be justified.[35]

---

33. The historic strategies of church-world encounter can be described as intra-institutional, counter-institutional, and para-institutional. The Lutheran doctrine of vocation expresses the first, the ecclesial social-action predispositions of Reformed and Roman Catholic traditions the second, and the left-wing Reformation traditions the third. See Gabriel Fackre, "IBM and the Incognito Christ," unpublished manuscript, Greenleaf Center.

34. Wolfhart Pannenberg, *Systematic Theology*, vol. 1, trans. Geoffrey Bromiley (Grand Rapids: Wm. B. Eerdmans, 1991), 155.

35. Ronald Thiemann, *Revelation and Theology: The Gospel as Narrated Promise* (Notre Dame, Ind.: University of Notre Dame Press, 1985), 154, 155.

Can it be said that here two Lutheran theologians of rather different persuasion (who make no reference to one another in their works on revelation) transpose the soteriological simultaneity of righteousness and sin into an epistemological simultaneity of trusting doctrinal assertions, but making no claim that they are knowledge? Influenced, of course, by other considerations — Pannenberg's commitment to a universal rationality and Thiemann's anti-foundationalism — nevertheless eschatology seems to function here for both as a counsel of modesty and recognition of ambiguity, kindred to the same cautions concerning the "having but not having" of *simul iustus et peccator*.[36] Also interesting, and possibly related to this question, is the fact that both Pannenberg and Thiemann have had important roles in the preparatory documents for two of the three ELCA proposals, Pannenberg on the condemnations and Thiemann as a Lutheran member of the four-year study team that prepared *A Common Calling*. Both reflect an ecumenical openness that coheres with their epistemological modesties.

Conclusion

The proposed new relationships are a teaching moment for the ELCA to bring its charism and concerns to its ecumenical agenda. Here may be a *kairos* for witness to justification by grace through faith that entails a haveability — yet one held, as at the communion rail, only in frail reaching hands. It certainly brings a needed Word for the three partners which Providence has put in long twentieth-century conversation with the ELCA. If possible, may that gift and admonition be gracefully given. And may the charisms and concerns of those same partners be gracefully received — the subject of my next lecture.

36. Another Lutheran, Søren Kierkegaard, attacked the epistemological certainties of Hegel and other nineteenth-century offerers of false security with a comparable understanding of the faith that "treads water over fifty thousand fathoms." How this Lutheran refrain of epistemological struggle, modesty, and ambiguity comports with the assurances of *capax* earlier discussed, and why the Pannenberg-Thiemann observations are posed as questions, is not clear.

Gifts Received:
Sovereignty and Sanctification

GABRIEL FACKRE

In the first lecture we listened for a word that others must hear
from the Lutheran tradition, the twofold word of haveability
and simultaneity, the *capax/simul* interpreting *justification*. Now
we turn to a word Lutherans must hear from others. It has to do
with justification by faith in the context of the majesty of God
over us, and the effects of the justifying grace of God imparted *to
us*. These emphases are not precluded by the Lutheran charism,
as the thread of mutual admonition in the documents behind the
present proposals indicate. Indeed, the stewardship of *sovereignty*
and *sanctification*, as I shall describe them, includes those ecumenical partners with whom the ELCA is now in conversation.

As noted in the first lecture, the legitimacy of mutual admonition presupposes mutual affirmation on basic commonalities. If *justification by grace through faith* is the article by which the
church stands or falls, its demonstrable presence must be established as a precondition for steps proposed. The ELCA has every
right to ask for explicit evidence of that premise in their partners'
texts and traditions. I reference these formal commitments in this
footnote.[1]

1. The twentieth-century exchange between Lutherans and Roman Cath-

For all the textual evidence, faithfulness to this article (as well as to other articles of basic Christian faith) is under serious erosion in the churches that formally espouse it. We are all in the same boat and there is no safe ecclesiastical harbor. However, the determination to retrieve the classical heritage shown by today's neo-confessional and centrist movements (to be dis-

---

olics on the doctrine of justification produced this "Common Statement" in the seventh round of the dialogue in North America: "It is only because Catholics and Lutherans share fundamental convictions regarding justification that they can be in increasing accord on criteria of Christian authenticity and accept justification as an *articulus stantis et cadentis ecclesiae* protective of the *solus Christus.* . . ." Paragraph 155, "Common Statement," *Justification by Faith: Lutherans and Catholics in Dialogue, VII,* ed. H. George Anderson, T. Austin Murphy, and Joseph H. Burgess (Minneapolis: Augsburg, 1985), 70. December 1998 is the date set for adoption of the more wide-ranging and binding "Joint Declaration on the Doctrine of Justification," now in a 1996 draft that has been declared by a joint Lutheran–Roman Catholic drafting group "adequate basis for future modifications" (Agenda, Meeting of the LWF Council, Geneva, Switzerland, 24 September–1 October, 1996, 2).

For the Episcopal Church, Articles XI-XIII of its "Thirty-nine Articles" set forth standard Reformation teaching on faith and works, with Article XI dealing specifically with justification: "We are accounted righteous before God, only for the merit of our Lord and Saviour Jesus Christ by Faith, and not for our own works or deservings." "Articles of Religion," *Book of Common Prayer* (New York: The Seabury Press, 1979), 870. While now defined in the *Book of Common Prayer* as an "historical document," the present status of which is unclear, the newly revised version of the Concordat endorses this statement: "We share a common understanding of God's justifying grace, i.e., that we are accounted righteous and made righteous before God only by grace through faith because of the merits of our Lord and Saviour Jesus Christ, and not on account of our works or merit." "Concordat of Agreement," *Lutheran-Episcopal and Lutheran Reformed Ecumenical Proposals:* Documents for Action by 1997 Churchwide Assembly (Chicago: Office of the Bishop [Department of Ecumenical Affairs] of the Evangelical Lutheran Church in America, 1996), 8.

All the Reformed Churches (PCUSA, RCA, UCC), reflecting their confessional documents, and after churchwide study, endorsed at their highest judicatory level the "Joint Statement on Justification" which asserts: "For Christ's sake we sinners have been reconciled to God, not because we earned God's acceptance but by an act of God's sheer mercy. . . . Those trusting in this gospel, believing in Christ as Saviour and Lord, are justified in God's sight. Both Lutheran and Reformed traditions confess this gospel in the language of justification by grace through faith alone." "Joint Statement on Justification,"

cussed in lecture three) converges exactly with the return to foundational texts and traditions in the 1997 proposals and is cause for hope that what we say is true in principle, is also increasingly true, in fact.[2]

Sovereignty

An improbable alliance of Roman Catholic, Reformed, and Anglican traditions has been noted by Robert Jenson in the earlier cited *Unbaptized God*. It emerges as a shared criticism of certain Lutheran teachings (illustrating the flawed doctrine of God in western Christendom, according to Jenson). For example, in the Reformed–Roman Catholic statement on the Real Presence there is a "specific if polite shared opposition to Lutheran innovations" expressed in the counterpoint assertion that

> the realization of the presence of Christ . . . is the proper work of the Holy Spirit, which takes place . . . as the Church calls upon the Father to send down the Holy Spirit to sanctify.[3]

Invitation to Action, ed. James E. Andrews and Joseph A. Burgess (Minneapolis: Fortress Press, 1984), 9. Those dubious about UCC confessional lore will want to read Charles Hambrick-Stowe's "Justification by Grace Through Faith: Views from the United Church of Christ," *Lutheran/Reformed Church Dialogue and the UCC* in *New Conversations* 10:2 (Winter/Spring 1988): 42-47, one of the papers written for reentry in 1988 of the UCC into the present negotiations. That same issue of *New Conversations* includes other essays on the United Church of Christ as a confessional church and on UCC polity.

When all is said and done about ecclesial texts and traditions, whether as historical or contemporary documents, we are reminded by the Lutheran and Catholic authors of the Common Statement "that in both of our churches the gospel has not always been proclaimed, that it has been blunted by reinterpretation, that it has been transformed by various means into self-satisfying systems of commands and prohibitions" (*Justification by Faith*, 74).

2. See the writer's overview article, "The Church of the Center," in *Interpretation* 51:2 (April 1997): 130-42, an issue devoted to the developing centrist/neoconfessional movements in mainline Protestantism.

3. Robert W. Jenson, *Unbaptized God: The Basic Flaw in Ecumenical Theology* (Minneapolis: Fortress Press, 1992), 130.

This coheres with a similar Anglican opposition to Lutheran premises in the Anglican–Roman Catholic eucharistic agreements:

> It is the Lord present at the right hand of the Father and *therefore transcending* the sacramental order, who thus offers to his church, in the eucharistic signs, the special gift of himself.[4] (emphasis added)

We find here a strong accent on the divine *sovereignty*, and the attendant work of the Holy Spirit to relate that to us, as a common eucharistic refrain of the ELCA's conversation partners, one juxtaposed to the Lutheran stress on the divine solidarity with us, as in its teaching on ubiquity.

Of course, sacramentology is not soteriology. But views of the eucharist do have a direct bearing on *how* justifying grace is understood to come to us. Thus we return to the central theme of justification by faith, but this time to read it in light of the partners' common accent on the "above and beyond" rather than the "in, with, and under."

The shared emphasis on the divine sovereignty occurs again in the way historic confessions and creeds are viewed by the partners, also carriers of the message of justification. Although described in different ways — from the *"semper reformanda"* of the Reformed heritage to the "development of doctrine" in Catholic traditions — the note of *unhaveability* is common to Reformed, Anglican, and Roman Catholic, a stress on *"new* light and truth" not overturning, but not confined to, the past doctrinal sedimentations. In these traditions, the sovereign God is always above or out ahead, calling the church to a reconsideration of its most prized inheritance.

---

4. Jenson, *Unbaptized God,* 130.

Confessions in the Reformed Tradition

Commenting on the different understandings of confessions, Karl Barth declares:

> To our fathers the historical past was something which called not for loving and devoted admiration but for careful and critical scrutiny. . . . There are documentary statements of their beliefs . . . but . . . our fathers had good reason for leaving us *no* Augsburg Confession authentically interpreting the word of God, *no* Formula of Concord, *no* "Symbolic Books" which might later, like the Lutheran, come to possess an odor of sanctity. . . . It *may* be our doctrinal task to make a careful revision of the theology of Geneva or the Heidelberg Catechism or of the Synod of Dort or . . . it *may* be our task to draw up a new creed. . . .[5]

Indeed, Barth speaks of these things in the same breath as the Reformed accent on the divine sovereignty, the *"Deo soli gloria"* and thus its "resolute refusal to deify any created thing . . . its *finitum non est capax infiniti.* . . ."[6] *A Common Calling*, the Lutheran-Reformed document that grounds the 1997 proposal of full communion, makes the same kind of distinction between Lutheran and Reformed views, but does so in the context of ecumenics rather than polemics;

> Since Lutherans have effectively elevated the ecumenical creeds and the confessions of the sixteenth century above later statements of faith, they have declined to add new documents to their confessional corpus. . . . By contrast, the Reformed communities have shown greater willingness to develop new confessions in response to contemporary problems and issues . . . asserting the principle *reformata semper reformanda.* . . .[7]

5. Karl Barth, *The Word of God and the Word of Man*, trans. Douglas Horton (Boston: The Pilgrim Press, 1928), 229, 230.
6. Barth, *The Word of God*, 231.
7. *A Common Calling*, 29.

The contrasting Reformed tradition can easily be seen in all three present conversation partners, each with their history of new confessions and statements of faith that seek to re-contextualize historic Christian beliefs. However, the Reformed efforts in re-formulation are not, in *A Common Calling*, polemicized, but placed in the setting of the counsel of "mutual admonition," arguing for each as a corrective to the reductionist temptations of the other.

Development of Doctrine in the Catholic Tradition

Roman Catholic

Avery Dulles summarizes the view of his church on the development of authoritative Christian teaching:

> Since John Henry Newman wrote his great *Essay on the Development of Doctrine* (1845), the idea that dogma "develops" has gained general acceptance in the Catholic church. . . . When a pope or ecumenical council defines a dogma, the resulting definition is a human formulation of revealed truth. Catholics accept such teaching as irreversibly true and in that sense ir-reformable. . . . [But] it is always possible to plumb the truth of revelation more deeply and to express it more aptly in relation to the needs and possibilities of new times and situations.[8]

This assertion is reflected in the *Catechism of the Catholic Church* under the heading "Growth in understanding of faith":

> Thanks to the assistance of the Holy Spirit, the understanding of both the realities and the words of the heritage of faith is able to grow in the life of the Church.[9]

8. Avery Dulles, "Faith and Revelation," in *Systematic Theology: Roman Catholic Perspectives*, vol. 1, ed. Francis Schüssler Fiorenza and John P. Galvin (Minneapolis: Fortress Press, 1991), 124.
9. Paragraph 94, *Catechism of the Catholic Church* (Liguori, Mo.: Liguori Publications, English translation, 1994), 29.

Comparably, Richard McBrien notes that *Mysterium Ecclesiae* (Congregation of the Doctrine of the Faith, 1973) is an important commentary on the Roman Catholic understanding of the development of doctrine, asserting that:

> Not every dogma was originally expressed in the best form. A dogma can reflect "the changeable conceptions of a given epoch" *(Mysterium Ecclesiae)* and "the expressive power of language used at a certain point in time" *(Mysterium Ecclesiae)*.[10]

While the deposit of dogma is considered "irreformable," the contextuality of its form is acknowledged and new interpretations allowed and expected. And more, the formulation of *new* dogma has and will take place, always, of course, within magisterial constraints.

Anglican

No statement on the re-forming of sixteenth-century confessions and catechesis appears in the *Concordat* equivalent to the statement cited earlier from *A Common Calling*. However, as noted, "The Articles of Religion," the doctrinal standards of the first (1549) *The Book of Common Prayer*, are located in the section of the current *The Book of Common Prayer: According to the Use of the Episcopal Church* described as "Historical Documents of the Church."[11] In the section immediately preceding the latter, appears "An Outline of the Faith Commonly Called the Catechism," showing additions to the doctrine found in "The Articles of Religion," arguably developments from trajectories within The Articles.[12] Other than a com-

---

10. Richard P. McBrien, *Catholicism,* Study Edition (Minneapolis: Winston Press, 1981), 71, 841.

11. *The Book of Common Prayer: According to the Use of the Episcopal Church* (New York: The Seabury Press, 1979).

12. New accents not precluded by earlier formulations, but arguably developments of themes earlier only implicit, included, for example, twentieth-century theological concerns about the created order and the struggle for justice

parison of this sort from within documents, there is no official statement on the development of doctrine in the Anglican communion.[13] Much evidence of the internal development discernible in doctrinal sections of *The Book of Common Prayer* can be adduced from the actual writing and practice of Anglican theologians — from reflections on Newman's famous essay and its implications to arguments for not only the development but the "remaking" of doctrine.[14] Thus in both the texts and traditions of the Episcopal Church, USA, the call for *aggiornamento* found in the Roman Catholic tradition also appears.

For all the differences in how the three traditions strive to protect doctrinal faithfulness over time — from return ever and again to the Word that addresses the Christian community to a magisterium privileged to discern that Word, or in the conceptual warrants for doctrinal change, ever-reforming or ever-developing, they share a readiness for additions to — or significant reinterpreta-

---

and peace, as reflected in the additions of God's intention as "harmony with creation." Other additions include: "we are called to enjoy [creation] and to care for it in accordance with God's purposes"; "revelation to Israel . . . to love justice, to do mercy, and to walk humbly with their God"; the commandment "to work and pray for peace . . . to be kind to all the creatures of God"; Christ coming so that "we may live in harmony with God, within ourselves, with our neighbors and with all creation"; a postmortem view of salvation (with religious pluralism in mind?) as the interpretation of Christ's descent into Hades: Christ "went to the departed and offered them the benefits of redemption; the "ministry of the laity . . . the ministry of lay persons is to represent Christ and his church; to bear witness to him wherever they may be; and, according to the gifts given to them, to carry on Christ's reconciliation in the world." Ibid., 845, 846, 849, 855.

Another aspect of the development of doctrine observable in comparing "An Outline of Faith" with "The Articles of Religion" is the diminishment and even disappearance of certain articles in the latter, as, for example, those on "sin" (IX, XV, XVI), salvation alone in Christ (XVIII), predestination and election (XVII) and, troubling for the Lutheran-Episcopal *Concordat*, "justification" (XI, XIII).

13. For a landmark Anglican struggle with these issues see Owen Chadwick's *From Bossuet to Newman: The Idea of Doctrinal Development* (Cambridge: Cambridge University Press, 1957). For an "evangelical Anglican" study of the issues and argument for development, see Peter Toon, *The Development of Doctrine in the Church* (Grand Rapids: Wm. B. Eerdmans, 1979).

14. As in Maurice F. Wiles, *The Remaking of Christian Doctrine* (Philadelphia: Westminster Press, 1978).

tions of — received texts. This distinguishes them functionally and formally from the Lutheran tradition's doctrinal self-definition in terms of a sixteenth-century Book of Concord to which no addition has been made, and from Lutheranism's suspicion of any effort at reformulation, as in the *variata* of the Augsburg Confession.

The partner commonalities here can be seen as the work of the same accent on the divine reserve about givens, the unhaveability of God, reflected in the shared eucharistic teaching on the divine transcendence and the necessary connecting work of the Holy Spirit. Yet rather than interpreting this difference as an unbridgeable chasm, the long ecumenical exchange of the ELCA with disparate traditions points toward a "mutual admonition" in which each pole, at the least, cannot afford to ignore the warnings by the other of reductionist temptations, and at most, learn something new from a neglected counterpoint.

Lutheran Learnings

I want to say briefly how the gift of its partners might be given to the ELCA — here the gift of sovereignty, later the gift of sanctification — but also look to some examples of mutuality, one in mission and another in a theologian who models "complementarity." First, to a case in point of the Lutheran need to hear the word of unhaveability, of the *non capax* of its partners in conversation.

A showcase of the unqualified deployment of the Lutheran *capax* can be found, I believe, in the mode of argument used by some Lutherans in their opposition to lifting the condemnations and to the Lutheran-Reformed *A Common Calling*. The parallel between the premises of the document *Outmoded Condemnations?* by the Göttingen Faculty of Theology[15] (respond-

15. Faculty of Theology, Georgia Augusta University, Göttingen, *Outmoded Condemnations? Antitheses Between the Council of Trent and the Reformation on Justification, The Sacrament and The Ministry — Then and Now,* trans. Oliver K. Olson with Franz Posset (Fort Wayne, Ind.: Luther Academy, 1992).

ing to *The Condemnations of the Reformation Era: Do They Still Divide?*)[16] and those of "A Review of 'A Common Calling'," by the Department of Systematic Theology of Concordia Theological Seminary,[17] is striking. Indeed Robert Preus played a role in the publication of the former and is one of the authors of the latter. *Outmoded Condemnations?* rightly identifies, formally, a crucial Reformation assertion: "The critical role of the Scripture over against the church is of the highest basic significance."[18] Yet, *functionally*, throughout the document, final appeal is made to a document of the church, *The Book of Concord*. This is in notable contrast to both the Lutheran–Roman Catholic and Lutheran-Reformed theological work which assessed respective ecclesial views on justification and the sacraments by biblical norms. Thus *Outmoded Condemnations?* demands exact conformity with the language of sixteenth-century texts:

> The hidden commonality which determines the complementarity behind the statements of both sides in the document is only presupposed and accepted on the basis of contemporary hermeneutical reflections, but not demonstrated on the basis of texts to be interpreted. If one works with the hermeneutical category "complementarity," one must first of all show that the texts themselves contain this focal point from which the divergent sides are developed.[19]

The same point is made in the rejection of *A Common Calling:*

> By acceding to this assumption, the Lutherans have, in effect, surrendered not only their understanding of the confessions as permanent statements of the truth, but also the claims which

16. *The Condemnations of the Reformation Era: Do They Still Divide?* ed. Kurt Lehmann and Wolfhart Pannenberg (Minneapolis: Fortress Press, 1990).
17. The Department of Systematic Theology, "A Review of 'A Common Calling,'" *Concordia Theological Review* 57:3 (July 1993): 193-213.
18. *Outmoded Condemnations?*, 4.
19. *Outmoded Condemnations?*, 14-15.

these confessions make for themselves as authoritative doctrine derived from the Scriptures as the Word of God.[20]

In both criticisms, the final court of appeal is the language of "the texts," the sixteenth-century "texts themselves." How is this faithful to the stated "critical role of Scripture against the church"? Rather, it is the assumption that the Lutheran confessions constitute a finite medium capable of receiving the Infinite, carrying forward in a body of written words the Word incarnate. A doctrine of the inerrancy of Scripture is a predictable corollary of the sacrality associated with written words, and such is found in these same quarters. In both cases, the needed emphasis of the Lutheran tradition on the *resource* role of Confessions in interpreting Scripture (the sole source of Christian teaching — *sola scriptura*) — needs to hear the counsel of *unhaveability* from its ecumenical partners. Indeed, the interpretation of historic confessions and condemnations as embodying mutually needed "emphases" and "concerns" in both the books reviewed is just that kind of proposal to bring together the "haveable" and the "unhaveable," continuity and discontinuity. It is no accident that Pannenberg and Thiemann, with their eschatological understandings of doctrine, have had important roles in writing the preparatory documents associated with both the lifting of the condemnations and the Covenant of Agreement.[21]

Sanctification

Of course sanctification is involved in justification, so far as the latter is the real and essential beginning of sanctification. Nevertheless sanctification is to be distinguished from justification. . . . justification is an act of God outwith man, by which

20. "A Review of 'A Common Calling,' " 197.
21. For a way of incorporating their eschatological interpretation of revelation, see Gabriel Fackre, *The Doctrine of Revelation: A Narrative Interpretation* (Edinburgh: The University of Edinburgh Press; Grand Rapids: Wm. B. Eerdmans, 1997), 217-23.

God assigns to him an alien righteousness; whereas sanctification is an activity of God in man's inward part.[22]

So Heinrich Heppe summarizes the refrain of the Reformed confessions, catechisms, and statements of faith, past and present. Reformed theology from Calvin forward put an emphasis on grace as power as well as pardon, growth in the Christian life as well as declaration of the unmerited favor of God toward the sinner. The righteousness of Christ is imparted as well as imputed to the believer, a *becoming* holy as well as, forensically, being declared holy.

Correlated to the promise of grace in our "inward part" is the call to obey the imperative, as well as joyfully receive the indicative, a "grateful obedience" as it is often described by the Reformed. Sanctification and its demands entail, therefore, without question, a "third use of the law" with its function of claiming and guiding the justified sinner in the life of good works.

The doctrinal statements of all the ELCA partners make a place for sanctification so understood. Thus the Westminster Confession:

> These good works, done in obedience to God's commandments, are the fruits and evidences of a true and lively faith; and by them believers manifest their thankfulness . . . their ability to do good works is not at all from themselves, but wholly from the Spirit of Christ.[23]

And in the *Articles of Religion,* after "by Faith only" comes:

> Albeit the Good Works which are the fruits of Faith, and follow after Justification, cannot put away our sins, and endure the severity of God's judgment; yet they are pleasing and acceptable to God in Christ, and do spring necessarily of a true and

22. Heinrich Heppe, *Reformed Dogmatics.* Revised and edited by Ernst Bizer. English trans., G. T. Thomson (Grand Rapids: Baker Book House, 1978), 565.
23. *The Westminster Confession of Faith,* 1647, XVI, 2, 3.

lively Faith, inasmuch that by them a lively Faith may be as evidently known as a tree discerned by fruit.[24]

Important differences exist between Reformation (Lutheran, Reformed, and Anglican) and Roman Catholic understandings of both justification and sanctification. However, on the matter at hand, Roman Catholicism joins Reformed and Anglican traditions in a stress on the grace at work in "the inward part" that makes for growth in the Spirit with its corresponding call to obedience:

> The Holy Spirit is the master of the interior life. By giving birth to the "inner man," justification entails the *sanctification* of his whole being. . . . Sanctifying grace is an habitual gift, a stable and supernatural disposition that perfects the soul itself to enable it to live with God, to act by his love.[25]

In the Roman Catholic–Lutheran discussions on justification, it has been acknowledged that there is "a clear difference" between an understanding of grace as

> an objective *reality* on God's side *"outside ourselves,"* and on the other hand as a *reality in the human soul*, a "quality" intrinsically "adhering" in the *human soul*. . . .[26]

with the counterpoint doctrine linking

> the righteousness of the believer with the righteousness of Christ *extra se* ("outside himself"), in which the believer participates, and yet at the same time [seeing] the justified person, as far as he himself is concerned, as still a sinner (*simul iustus et peccator*, at once righteous and sinner). . . .[27]

---

24. *The Book of Common Prayer*, 870.
25. *Catechism of the Catholic Church*, paragraphs 1995 and 2000, 483, 484.
26. *The Condemnations of the Reformation Era: Do They Still Divide?*, 47.
27. Ibid., 47.

But Lutherans speak of "sanctification," too. After canvassing the history in and beyond Lutheranism of separating justification and sanctification, especially so in conceptions of the *ordo salutis*, Gerhard Forde in *Christian Dogmatics* declares,

> Only one way remains open: to grasp justification and sanctification as a dynamic unity in the light of the eschatological nature of the divine action. Justification by faith means the death of the old and the resurrection of the new. Sanctification is what results when that is done to us.[28]

A new self *theologically* comes to be in justification, and with it *anthropologically*, a new self in sanctification.

> If justification is unconditional and total, it explodes into love and good works. If not, it simply leaves the self to contend with its own righteousness and despair.[29]

Thus, Lutherans also hold to sanctification, as is reiterated in all the documents preparatory to the current decisions.[30]

However, the warnings against the *ordo salutis*,[31] the denial of sanctification as "progress," the construal of the Christian life as a never-ending struggle, the questions raised both about a "third use of the law" and the language of "cooperation," the historic Lutheran challenge to the Roman Catholic view of "infused grace" — all point to a different reading of sanctification. The difference lies at two points:

1. The decisiveness of justification both before God and in the depths of the new person — from "the death of the old to the rebirth of the new" — is such that "the spontaneity and *hilaritas*

28. Gerhard Forde, "Justification and Sanctification," *Christian Dogmatics*, vol. 2, ed. Carl E. Braaten and Robert W. Jenson (Philadelphia: Fortress Press, 1984), 430.

29. Forde, "Justification," 434.

30. As in 4.7, "The Good Works of the Justified" in the working document of *Joint Declaration on the Doctrine of Justification*, 7.

31. "The attempt to set it forth as an 'order' . . . is disastrous." Forde, 428.

. . . of faith"[32] will "explode . . . in good works." To the extent that there is a new self, how can it not evidence the fruits of that newness? The new self does not need to be told what to do (no domineering "third use of the law"), for it does spontaneously (sanctification) what its new state (justification) entails.

2. Yet the old self hangs on:

> The simultaneity of sin and righteousness as total states is the *actual* situation revealed by divine justification. The divine act itself shatters all human presumption about progress and process. God has something else in mind.[33]

To the latter assertion, the question comes from the ELCA partners: Is all belief in "progress" in the Christian life only "human presumption"? And to the former another question must be put: Is the spontaneity and *hilaritas* a too-simple assumption about the *haveability* of a new state of being, one innocent of the needs of the law's mandates and guidelines in the life of the believer?

Lutheran Learnings

Where *simultaneity* is asserted unqualifiedly, "mutual admonition" from ELCA partners must be heard:

1. The stress on the persistence of sin in the life of the justified can become *the* characterization of the Christian life. When this emphasis alone is heard, the *possibilities* of advance in the Christian life as warranted by sanctifying grace are muted or missing. The reminder of these possibilities is the gift given by the self-defined sanctification traditions of the three ELCA conversation partners.

2. The trust that justification is in "dynamic unity" with sanctification in such wise that good works flow spontaneously from the new state can obscure the mandate that goes with a divine sovereignty, always beyond, claiming the believer for

32. Forde, "Justification," 427.
33. Ibid., 407.

further steps on the journey. The reminder of this distance — the *non capax* — is the gift brought by the stewards of the *sanctification,* now in the imperative mood, stressing the importance of the third use of the law.

But let us cast these admonitions differently by seeing how they may work in conjunction with counterpoint Lutheran admonitions.

Mutualities in Mission

Where one, or some, or all, of the proposals are accepted by the ELCA, significant new possibilities in mission open up. As mentioned in my first lecture, the receiving of a partner's charisms and concerns carries with it fuller Christian teaching within the church. The same is true in mission beyond the doors of the church. A case in point is the deepening of the church's *social mission.* Stewart Herman has sought to show this in a paper on Lutheran critical appropriation of the Reformed theme of "covenant."[34] Here, I will speak about it in terms of the motifs under discussion.

The outworking of sovereignty and sanctification in the social mission of the three Lutheran partners can be seen in their respective histories of church involvement in efforts at systemic change. The sovereignty of Christ over the marketplace and countinghouse, as well as the church and the soul, and the associated imperative for Christ's church, *as church,* to set up signs there to his regency, mark these three traditions as "world-formative" in intention (Nicholas Wolterstorff's words). And sanctification in the same traditions reinforces that intention, by giving hope that genuine social change can be achieved. Where the Lutheran tradition of two kingdoms, the unchallengeability of society's orders, and the radicality of the fall leads to an uncritical acceptance of the status quo and a retreat to personal or ecclesial interiorities, the partners' witness is a needed word.

34. Stewart W. Herman, unpublished and untitled draft, 12/10/1996.

While this ecclesial momentum in and hope for secular structures are gifts to be received, the giving goes both ways. Lutheran sobriety about sin knows of the corruptibility of every system and every presumed social advance, as well as the sin in every ecclesial effort at transformation, as in the theocratic impulses of Geneva, Canterbury, and Rome. Further, its accent on the divine solidarity is a worthy testimony to the role of social systems as stabilizing orders of preservation, which also exist to set bounds to human sin. Solidarity makes its witness to others also in the Lutheran doctrine of vocation which looks to the individual Christian believer to be "a Christ to the neighbor" *within* the structures and orders of society.

When the accents we have been examining are seen to be mutually corrective rather than intrinsically conflictive, the social mission of partnered churches could bring together: (1) two historic Christian approaches to social change — the systemic "counter-institutional" tradition of the ELCA partners, and the "intra-institutional" Lutheran tradition of Christian vocation within social-political systems; (2) the impetus to church involvement in systemic change and hope for advance therein, yet the realism about what, in fact, can be achieved in society and a proper self-criticism of the church itself as an agent of change.

Reinhold Niebuhr:
The Meeting of Mutual Admonitions

The "Lutheran Reinhold Niebuhr" is a not uncommon description of this influential twentieth-century theologian. Thus "Niebuhr for the 90s? Toward a Lutheran Revival" is vigorously argued by Mark Ellingsen in the *Lutheran Forum*.[35] Yet Langdon Gilkey can say,

---

35. Mark Ellingsen, "Niebuhr for the 90s? Toward a Lutheran Revival," *Lutheran Forum* 27:2 (May 1993): 40-43. See also the positive response by Todd Murken, "The Atonement in Reinhold Niebuhr's Theology of History," 10-13.

Because it was in a humanistic, moralistic, and optimistic culture that Niebuhr emphasized sin and justification, he was mistaken as "merely a Lutheran" who separated law and gospel so far as to be unable to bring them together again. No interpretation of Niebuhr could be further from the truth. . . . As with Calvin, justification in Niebuhr is teleological, leading to a more fruitful moral and political existence . . . all the Calvinistic moral and political passion and implicitly moral and political teleology in time was in him.[36]

Gilkey is echoing in this "teleology in time" the Reformed admonition vis-à-vis sanctification. However, such was never in Niebuhr separated from the Lutheran caution that every pious and political advance is subject to corruption. Here is an example of ecumenical complementarity.

Niebuhr's effort to bridge historic differences reflects his own ecclesial history, a factor often ignored in the interpretation of his theology and ethics.[37] Raised in the Evangelical Synod of North America and influential in the merger of that church with the Reformed Church in the U.S. in 1934, he was shaped by their three symbols, the Augsburg Confession, Luther's Small Catechism, and the Heidelberg Catechism. His explicit criticisms of both Calvinism and Lutheranism reflect this familiarity with them and his effort to learn from this laboratory of coexistence. Yet other aspects of his ecclesial history may also have a bearing on the three ELCA conversation partners: Niebuhr's Anglican spouse, Ursula (deceased January 10, 1997), and his later growth in appreciation of aspects of the Roman Catholic tradition.

36. Langdon Gilkey, "Reinhold Niebuhr's Theology of History," *The Journal of Religion* 54 (1974): 384.

37. A point I argue in my introduction to his life and thought, *The Promise of Reinhold Niebuhr*, rev. ed. (Lanham, Md.: University Press of America, 1994).

Correction and Complementarity

In a key section of the second volume of the Gifford lectures, Niebuhr explores "Grace as Power In, and as Mercy Towards, Man."[38] For Niebuhr, the Christian life is grounded in *Christus pro nobis*, the mercy of God declared in Christ, the pardon offered to sinners accomplished on, and declared by, the cross. Justification is the unmerited favor of God received in faith. *Christus in nobis* is inextricable from *Christus pro nobis*. Saving grace is power as well as pardon, a new self with the possibilities of new growth and under the mandate to live in accord with the self's new state.

Concurrent with Niebuhr's probes of imputation and impartation in the Christian life, is the transposition of this partnership to the public sphere. Thus the assurance of grace as favor toward the sinner has its counterpart in the confidence that God will accomplish the divine purposes in public history, not penultimately where the struggle goes on without end, but ultimately, as expressed in the biblical images of the resurrection of the dead and a new heaven and a new earth. All is of grace as "favor" and not human works, in both the redeemed self and the eschatological society. It can only be so, for sin persists, and every stage of history is subject to its corruptions. Yet within history, as within the Christian life, grace is at work in the possibilities of advance, a grace of both gift and demand, with their indicatives and imperatives.

The "paradox" in Niebuhr's language of both/and, of what he describes as "having and not having," is regularly destroyed by reductionist readings of the Christian life and of human history. Thus in an historical setting of "optimism" and "moralism," Niebuhr brought to the fore the Lutheran *simultaneity of sin*. Regarding personal Christian life,

---

38. Reinhold Niebuhr, *The Nature and Destiny of Man*, vol. 2: *Human Destiny* (New York: Charles Scribner's Sons, 1945), 107-26.

the theologies which have sought to do justice to the positive aspects of regeneration have usually obscured the realities of sin which appear at every new level of virtue.[39]

So Niebuhr's respect for the profundity of Luther:

The saints are always intrinsically sinners; that is why they are declared righteous extrinsically . . . we are sinners in reality but are righteous in hope.[40]

"The theologies" that have obscured this realism are those that accent *sanctification* in both the Christian life and in history at large. They run from "sectarian" to Roman Catholic. Also Calvin, developing "his own doctrine of sanctification . . . arrives at conclusions hardly to be distinguished from Catholic ones."[41] In all cases, the problem is that

the Christian, in whom sin is broken "in principle," claims that the sins which remain are merely incidental "carnal desires" without recognizing that the sin of self-love is present in its more basic form . . . no longer subject to the paradox of having and not having it.[42]

Here we have "the Lutheran Niebuhr" asserting that, while in a new context that Lutherans have called *peccatum regnatum*,[43] a mighty struggle with even this "controlled sin" goes on in the life of the justified. This Lutheran emphasis is a corrective to the

---

39. Niebuhr, *Nature and Destiny*, vol. 2, 125.
40. Luther, *Works*, ed. Ficker, II, 104, 105, 176, quoted by Niebuhr on 124-25.
41. Niebuhr, *Nature and Destiny*, vol. 2, 199.
42. Ibid., 200.
43. "Controlled sin," as in the explanation of the new state in Appendix 1 of the *Joint Declaration of the Doctrine of Justification*, citing the commentary of a Joint Committee of the Evangelical Lutheran Church in Germany, *Agenda, Meeting of the LWF Council* (Geneva, Switzerland, 24 September–1 October 1996), 13.

sanctification traditions, as in Calvinism, where there is assumed the presence of a *"prevailing inclination . . .* to submit to his will"[44] with its tendency to perfectionism, moralism, self-righteous fury, and legalism. And in Niebuhrian transposition from self to society: history's genuine steps forward (his Reformed bequest) are accompanied by commensurate temptations and corruptibility that preclude the utopianisms and fanaticisms of automatic-progress theories.

But what of the mutuality of admonition? Niebuhr's admonishments of Lutheranism grow out of the sanctification and sovereignty aspects of his thought. In the

> Lutheran Reformation . . . the conscience is made uneasy about the taint of sin in all human enterprise; but the conviction that any alternative to a given course of action would be equally tainted, and that in any case the divine forgiveness will hallow and sanctify what is, really only eases the conscience prematurely.[45]

Grace is growth in and possibility for, as well as mercy toward, the believing sinner. In the same way, history itself has "indeterminate possibilities" obscured by the Lutheran emphasis on the persisting sin uncovered at "the ultimate level of religious judgment." The profound insight into universal corruptibility, when the only note struck, fails to incorporate "the prophetic note in Scripture" that distinguishes the worse from lesser sins, as in "the rich and powerful, the mighty and noble, the wise and the righteous," and thus "imperils and seems to weaken all moral judgments which deal with the 'nicely calculated less and more' of justice and goodness as revealed in the relativities of history,"[46] temptations of Lutheranism, related as they are to its two-kingdom ethic and separation of law from gospel.

44. Niebuhr, *Nature and Destiny,* vol. 2, 200.
45. Ibid., 196.
46. Reinhold Niebuhr, *The Nature and Destiny of Man,* vol. 1 (New York: Charles Scribner's Sons, 1945), 222, 221.

As well as recourse to the sanctification traditions in criticizing both Luther and "orthodox Lutheranism," Niebuhr deploys the accents of the *sovereignty* traditions to defend the role of radical imperatives in both personal and public life. He thus faults Lutheranism for quietistic tendencies that derive not only from a too-exclusive use of the *simul* in its view of society, but also the unqualified application there of its law-gospel distinction, its doctrine of orders, and its "left hand of God" ethics. In the motifs we have been examining here, it might be said that the Lutheran *capax* is too easily affiliated with the sociopolitical givens, especially so with the political "powers that be," with warrants sought in Romans 13. The corrective of *sovereignty* means that radical demands of Christ extend over the sociopolitical givens and are not limited to the believer or church. Thus Niebuhr challenged Luther's assertion that in the civil order "nothing *must be known* concerning the conscience, the Gospel, grace, remission of sins, heavenly righteousness or Christ himself; but Moses only and the works thereof," declaring

> the Kingdom of God and the demands of perfect love are . . . relevant to every political system and impinge on every social situation in which the self seeks to come to terms with the claims of other life.[47]

Niebuhr gave credit especially to the later Calvin and later Calvinists (Cromwell) for working out the public claims of the divine regency, as in movements for democracy and social justice. However, expressing their insights as a corrective rather than a replacement of Lutheran sobriety about what may be achieved in the public realm and the function of the orders as the restraint of sin, he spoke of them as discovering that it was "as important to place the ruler under the judgment of God as to regard him as an instrument of God for checking individual sin."[48]

Niebuhr's accent on the divine sovereignty is also, arguably,

47. Niebuhr, *The Nature and Destiny of Man*, vol. 2, 192.
48. Ibid., 221.

at work in his critique of Luther's confidence in an "ecstatic" faith that needs no urging to bring forth the works of love. Niebuhr judges that Luther's "Christ-mysticism" prompts him to declare that the soul of the believer is "so united with Christ that all his virtues flow into it,"[49] thus failing to see the need for the imperatives of law in the Christian life. But this criticism can also be seen as stemming from a Reformed accent on the divine sovereignty not contained in, but transcending and claiming from beyond the finite medium of the believer's heart through the third use of the law.[50]

Conclusion

Where the theme of mutual instruction and admonition appears in the preparatory documents, it is sometimes observed that the historic teachings of the respective churches on controverted questions do not reject what other churches affirm, but do reject what those churches deny. That is, in our theses at hand, insofar as the respective assertions about justification are not *reduced* to the accented motifs of what we have called *solidarity* and *simultaneity*, or *sovereignty* and *sanctification*, a rare moment of mutual teaching and learning is possible. Well said. Yet, in addition to that, can Lutherans and their partners accept the proposition that "the other" is *also* right in the different motifs it *affirms?* So considered, "mutual affirmation" takes on a deeper meaning than the discernment of necessary commonalities. It means also the affirmation of the others' charisms and concerns, and readiness to receive them. This year and next will tell the story of whether we are ready for such a step toward a church truly "catholic, evangelical, and ecumenical."

49. Ibid., 185.
50. On the function of the Reformed sovereignty in Niebuhr's theology on this point as well as others, see the writer's "Reinhold Niebuhr as a Reformed Theologian," in *Reformed Theology in America*, ed. David Wells (Grand Rapids: Wm. B. Eerdmans, 1985).

The Congregation and
the Unity of the Church

GABRIEL FACKRE

The *satis est* of the Augsburg Confession plays a prominent role in ELCA ecumenics. In the quest for fresh entry points to the discussion of the 1997 votes, I want to examine Article VII from the point of view of *the congregation*.

What is the church? —

[The church is] the assembly of all believers among whom the Gospel is preached in its purity and the holy Sacraments are administered according to the Gospel. For it is sufficient for the true unity of the Christian church that the Gospel be preached in conformity with a pure understanding of it and the sacraments be administered in accordance with the divine Word.[1]

Formally, this definition has to do with the church universal, the community of believers that was, is, and will be, over time and

---

1. Article VII [The Church], *The Augsburg Confession* (German translation), in *The Book of Concord: The Confessions of the Evangelical Lutheran Church,* trans. and ed. Theodore G. Tappert in collaboration with Jaroslav Pelikan, Robert Fisher, and Arthur Piepkorn (Philadelphia: Fortress Press, 1959), 32.

place and into eternity. Functionally — by associating "assembly" with preaching and sacramental acts — *church* in Article VII means the historical *congregation*. Luther has that locale in mind in the *Large Catechism* when he explains the Creed's "holy Christian church":

> The word *ecclesia* means an assembly. . . . We who assemble select a special place and give the house its name by virtue of the assembly. Thus the word "church" *(Kirche)* really means nothing else than a common assembly.[2]

The Holy Spirit "calls" and "gathers" believers into the church catholic and "enlightens" and "sanctifies" them in the same through the Word preached and sacraments celebrated in local assemblies . . . in living congregations. Augustana so interpreted, and Luther so appropriated, return us to the New Testament givens, the congregations with whom the apostles corresponded — Rome, Corinth, Ephesus, and those over whom the angels hovered, Smyrna, Sardis, Laodicea — gatherings brought to be by the Holy Spirit, but not without the tares among the wheat.

The focus on the congregation is not some Protestant primitivism, as a study of trends in Roman Catholic ecclesiology will show. So the important words of ecumenist George Tavard, speaking at a gathering on the ELCA ecumenical agenda and interpreting the ecclesiological implications of the second Vatican Council:

> Where it finds the Eucharist, it finds the church. . . . The Reformation focussed attention on two marks, notes, or signs, of the church: "where the Word is preached and the sacraments are administered according to the gospel." This was in fact an amplification of the definition of the church by Thomas Aquinas: The church is the gathering of the faithful *(congregatio fidelium)*. Aquinas and medieval theology in general did not define the church by the hierarchy or *magisterium*. This is a later

2. Martin Luther, *The Large Catechism*, in *The Book of Concord*, 416.

point of view, typical of the Counter-Reformation. . . . Defining the church by the faithful implicitly raises the question of what makes the faithful? They are faithful because they have heard the Word of God in the Holy Spirit, and they have been led by it to Christ, present among us in the Eucharist. . . . The fundamental ecclesiology is that the church is the communion of the faithful, gathered in Christ through the Holy Spirit.[3]

The congregation of Word and sacrament is a form of church life close to the heart of the Great Tradition.

Congregations are the focus of new attention today. Their durability, influence, and growth are factors in this fresh interest. While denominations downsize and vaunted paraparochial experiments disappear, the "body of 'people who regularly gather to worship in a particular place'" [the definition of a congregation by historians Wind and Lewis][4] survives, and in many places gives evidence of vitality. A new discipline of "congregational studies" emerges and vigorous institutions appear to service and "transform" congregations, e.g. the Alban Institute.[5] What are the ecumenical implications of the congregation, understood in both its classical doctrinal and contemporary empirical significance?

Such a question converges with the rising chorus of voices that are asking for new approaches to ecumenism, ones that go

3. George Tavard, "Ecumenical Perspectives on the Leuenberg Agreement," *The Leuenberg Agreement and Lutheran-Reformed Relationships,* ed. William G. Rusch and Daniel F. Martensen (Minneapolis: Augsburg, 1989), 121, 122. In a similar vein, see also Susan K. Wood, "Communion Ecclesiology: Source of Hope, Source of Controversy," *Pro Ecclesia* 2:4 (Fall 1993): 424-32. See especially: "There is a density of ontological realism here that extends not only to the sacramental realism of the presence of Christ under the species of bread and wine, but also a sacramental realism of the church, for where the Eucharist is, there is the church. There is an intrinsic relationship between the historical Christ, the sacramental Christ and the ecclesial Christ" (425).

4. *American Congregations,* vol. 1: *Portraits of Twelve Religious Communities,* ed. James P. Wind and James W. Lewis (Chicago: University of Chicago Press, 1994), 1.

5. Note especially the writings of Loren Mead, *The Once and Future Church* and *Transforming Congregations for the Future.*

beyond the current denominationally grounded efforts, as in Mark Heim's suggestions for a new start based on the realities of diverse traditions rather than denominations, or Teresa Berger's plea for a contextual ecumenism.[6] Rather than juxtapose alternative ecumenical entry points to current ones, however, I want to ask how an "ecumenism from below" based on the reality of the congregation might fructify hard-won advances in denominationally oriented ecumenics, especially bilaterals. Specifically, what import would the recovery of a congregation-grounded reading of Augustana VII have for 1997 decisions?

To answer that question I want to begin by taking a frank look at the theological state of affairs in American congregations.

Ecclesial Realities

"A Pallid but Personable Faith?" — asked the *Time* headline about a 1980 report on what North American congregations sought in their clergy.[7] Similar assessments and much sharper indictments of mainline Protestant faith and theology have been familiar themes since. Leander Keck said it as well as any in his widely read Beecher lectures. In many mainline congregations

> the theocentric praise of God has been displaced by anthropocentric utilitarianism. What matters most is that everyone get something out of the service, as the phrase goes. . . . In this inversion, the living God, whose biblical qualities like jealousy and wrath have been tamed, has been deprived of freedom, and having been reduced to the Great Enabler, has little to do except warrant our causes and help us fulfill our aspira-

6. S. Mark Heim, "The Next Ecumenical Movement," *The Christian Century* 113:24 (Aug. 12-21, 1996): 780-83; Teresa Berger, "Ecumenism: Postconfessional? Consciously Contextual?" *Theology Today* 53:2 (July 1996): 213-19.

7. *Time* (September 29, 1980), 85.

tions. . . . The opening line of the Westminster Confession is now reversed, for now the chief end of God is to glorify us and to be useful to us indefinitely.[8]

Keck believes the decline of mainline denominations is related to this anthropocentric turn:

Something is indeed amiss when a major denomination loses 245 members a day for more than twenty years, an aggregate of two million persons. Nor is it irrelevant that for every person from a nonreligious background who joins a mainline church, three leave for no church at all.[9]

If mainline congregations are captive to their culture and on the decline, what of the fast-growing "evangelical empire"?[10] According to one of its leading theologians, David Wells, contemporary evangelicals are hostage to the same anthropocentrism. Describing it as a "self-piety," dramatically illustrated in the success-oriented feel-good megachurches, he says:

Christian beliefs have mostly been retained, but they are not allowed to encumber the search for new forms of spirituality, technique and community. . . . The powerful vision of a humanity corrupted by sin being released to stand before God in all his glory . . . is now dying. It is being edged out by the small and tawdry interest of the self in itself, the self standing in the inner counsels of its own piety, the one hand bargaining with the other. . . .[11]

8. Leander Keck, *The Church Confident* (Nashville: Abingdon Press, 1993), 34, 35.

9. Keck, *Church Confident*, 21-22.

10. I am using "evangelical" in the sense designated in lecture one, the sixteenth-century Reformation principles, formal and material, intensified and internalized through the movements of pietism, Wesleyanism, the Awakenings, revivalism, and modernist-fundamentalist controversy.

11. David Wells, *No Place for Truth* (Grand Rapids: Wm. B. Eerdmans, 1993), 110, 185.

On these matters, what of the congregations involved in current bilateral negotiations with the ELCA — for example, the UCC, PCUSA, and ECUSA? We have some specific data on them. The Search Institute's recent study of "Effective Christian Education" in North American congregations rates the UCC as next to the lowest of the denominations surveyed in "Faith Maturity," and lowest in "Growth in Faith Maturity," with the Presbyterian Church, USA the next to the lowest in "congregational loyalty."[12] In a similar vein, Loren Mead's comparative studies show the pattern of decline of the denominations with whom the ELCA is contemplating communion, those covered in his research being the Episcopal, Presbyterian, and UCC Churches.[13]

And the ELCA? The same studies are revealing. In the Search Institute findings the ELCA is the very lowest in "Faith Maturity" — just underneath the UCC, next to lowest in "Growth in Faith Maturity," and lowest in "congregational loyalty" — just beneath the Presbyterians. In the Mead studies, the ELCA follows the general pattern, prompting the author's comment:

> Note that the curves are relatively congruent in shape and direction. They go up and down at similar points along the scale of years.[14]

George Lindbeck's observation is to the point. He says that the ELCA is

> swayed by the same current fashions and is not notably better rooted in the historic faith . . . the ELCA like other denominations, appears to be capitulating to the *Zeitgeist* and losing the struggle for confessional integrity for the foreseeable future.[15]

12. Peter L. Benson and Carolyn H. Elkin, *Effective Christian Education: A Summary Report on Faith, Loyalty and Congregational Life* (Minneapolis: Search Institute, 1990), 41.

13. Loren Mead, *Transforming Congregations for the Future* (New York: The Alban Institute, 1994), 3-5.

14. Mead, *Transforming Congregations*, 5.

15. George A. Lindbeck, "The Church Faithful and Apostate: Reflections on Kansas City," *Lutheran Forum* 28:1 (Lent 1994): 12.

For Lutherans and others who might look to the historic episcopate as a bulwark against this cultural accommodation, Episcopal theologian Philip Turner's study of the same is instructive:

> The history traced above suggests a disturbing possibility, namely that forms like the historic episcopate, or the shape of the liturgy or the *Augsburg Confession* can remain in place yet be ignored or subverted or denied from below. If doctrine and discipline can be ignored or subverted in this way, and if the moral tradition that makes oversight and discipline possible falls into decline, the much to be desired ecumenical event of full communion between the ECUSA and the ELCA, may still leave the question of the apostolic succession in its proper sense unresolved.[16]

What is to be done? I believe there are some road signs to the way out of captivity. Ironically, they point back to the same location that illustrates the problem: the congregation.

Counter-signs

The groundbreaking Wind-Lewis study of the history of representative North American congregations demonstrates the chameleon-like tendencies of congregational life over time, too quickly adapting to cultural forces and accommodating regularly to society's premises and values. However, the same study shows that the congregation as worshiping community with a transcendent Referent provides traction against a slide into cultural givens, a finding consonant with Barth's observation that believ-

16. Philip Turner, "Episcopal Oversight and Ecclesiastical Discipline: On the Decline of a Practice," *Pro Ecclesia* 3:4 (Fall 1994). The postmodern "Rave Mass" conducted recently in the basement of Grace Cathedral, San Francisco, Matthew Fox preaching, is an example of Turner's point. See *Forum Letter* 24:3 (March 1995), which rightly links it with similar examples in both the UCC and the ELCA.

ers each Sunday are not allowed to forget that they are account-
able to Another. And more, the same study shows that the congregation is the principal steward of the church's theological
identity. Peter Berger, well-known for his early indictments of
local congregations,[17] said subsequently:

> What the church is all about is that one old story of God's
> dealings with [us], the story that spans the Exodus and Easter
> morning. When all is said and done the Christian community
> consists of those people who keep on telling this story to each
> other. . . .[18]

Continuing the narrative metaphor, the congregation is the basic
locale for telling and celebrating the Christian story. Here is the
place where, in season and out, the Word is preached and the
sacraments administered, and by the grace of God, rightly so.
For all its manifest flaws, this assembly is the basic bearer of the
promises of God to this people of God.

Evidence mounts of the refocus today in congregations on
that Story, a countercurrent to the Babylonian captivity earlier
noted. Preaching is enjoying a small renascence, and with it the
growing use of the lectionary and its requirement to attend to
the whole Tale. The teaching of Christian basics as well as the
growth of Bible study groups — even a revival of catechesis —
comes further to the fore as laity press for understanding their
identity vis-à-vis the ideologies and religious passions of the
hour.[19] Thus both the form of the congregation with its defining

17. Peter Berger, *The Noise of Solemn Assemblies* (Garden City, N.Y.: Dou-
bleday & Co., 1961).

18. Peter Berger, "A Call for Authority in the Christian Community," *The
Christian Century* 88:43 (October 27, 1971): 1262. For the heated 1960s debate on
the viability of the congregation, see the writer's argument for its necessary role
in "telling the story" in "The Crisis of the Congregation: A Debate," in *Voluntary
Associations: Essays in Honor of James Luther Adams*, ed. D. B. Robertson (Rich-
mond: John Knox Press, 1966), 275-98.

19. On the return of theology to Christian education see the issue
"Theology and Christian Education," *Christian Education Journal* 15:3 (Spring

marks of *kerygma* and *leitourgia* — Word and sacrament — and the biblical and doctrinal content now increasingly in evidence in many congregations, are countervailing signs among us.

The Pastor and the Reclaiming of Faith

Within congregations the office of pastor is established for special responsibilities:

> *Presbyters* serve as pastoral ministers of Word and sacraments in a local eucharistic community. They are preachers and teachers of the faith, exercise pastoral care, and bear responsibility for the discipline of the congregation to the end that the world may believe and that the entire membership of the Church may be renewed, strengthened and equipped in ministry.[20]

The life of the congregation and the ministry of the whole people of God require a special stewardship of the church's theological identity, and thus the ordination to ministry of Word and sacrament, and the regular telling and celebrating of the Christian story in the midst of a local people and place by the local pastor.

It is no accident that the erosion of theological identity earlier cited has produced a countermovement among *pastors*. These "presbyters" are at the forefront of movements of "reclaiming the faith" in mainline denominations, efforts described variously as neo-confessional and "centrist" (Christ, not the ideologies of

---

1995). On the revival of catechesis, see the symposium on the subject as it pertains to the *Catechism of the Catholic Church* in *Theology Today* 53:2 (July 1996): 148-76. The interest in catechism goes well beyond the Roman Catholic Church, as for example the work in the PCUSA in this country and the EKU in Europe on a new catechism, and the plans of the Confessing Christ in the UCC to develop a catechism for congregations. On the concern for basics in congregations see Dorothy and Gabriel Fackre, *Christian Basics* (Grand Rapids: Wm. B. Eerdmans, 1994).

20. "Ministry," *Baptism, Eucharist and Ministry,* Faith and Order Pamphlet No. 111 (Geneva: WCC, 1982), 27.

left and right as "center," and the doctrinal "centralities" retrieved). Whether structured in movements, or appearing as an emerging mindset, centrist/neoconfessional ferment is a direct challenge to the mainline church accommodation to culture. Note the recent commentary on this development: Jack Rogers' description and interpretation in his recent book, *Claiming the Center: The Christian Century* current tracking of "center" developments; the Lilly Foundation's sponsorship of the three-year research project of D. Jacobsen and W. Trollinger, "Re-forming the Center"; the journal of Bible and theology, *Interpretation*, devoting its April 1997 issue to "the center."[21] The ELCA was one of the first North American churches to create a platform for neoconfessional voices, as in its "Call to Faithfulness" conferences. This phenomenon has implications for ecumenism and specifically for ELCA relationships.[22]

The confessional/center development is to be distinguished from the "biblical renewal" movements that appeared in mainline denominations in the late 1970s, the latter often triggered by culture-war issues such as homosexuality and abortion and tied to inerrantist or infallibilist interpretations of Scripture.[23] In contrast, the former are focused on *theological* issues and *doctrinal* reference points that give the church an independent identity, and therefore strive not to be defined by culture-war questions with their Left-Right polarities. This does not preclude strong social justice commitments in the neoconfessional/center movements, but they do not follow party lines, striving for the freedom

21. Jack Rogers, *Claiming the Center* (Louisville: Westminster/John Knox, 1995). Douglas Jacobsen and William Vance Trollinger, Jr.'s "Evangelical and Ecumenical: Re-forming the Center," *The Christian Century* 111:21 (July 13-20, 1994): 682-83 is a commentary reflecting their Re-forming the Center project. The April 1997 issue of *Interpretation* includes an overview article by this writer, and essays by Jacobsen, William Abraham, and Mary Stewart Van Leeuwen.

22. There is an interesting overlap of leadership in these movements and a vigorous commitment to one or another, or all, of the proposed ELCA partnerships.

23. For the characteristics of, and distinctions within, evangelicalism, see the writer's *Ecumenical Faith in Evangelical Perspective* (Grand Rapids: Wm. B. Eerdmans, 1993).

under the Word that marked the Barmen declaration whose ca-
dences appear regularly in these circles. Further, the schismatic
tendency to which the movements of the 1970s were, and con-
tinue to be, prone is disavowed by confessional centrists who
strive to make their witness within existing structures. Many
"ecumenical evangelicals," however, are associated with the con-
fessional/center movements and mindset, finding unity with
"evangelical ecumenicals" in a common focus on foundational
Christian teaching.[24]

To explore the significance of this kind of grassroots neo-
confessionalism, I draw on my own experience in the "Confessing Christ" movement in the United Church of Christ that in-
volves over a thousand pastors. Its 1993 invitation letter strikes
characteristic notes:

> We believe that the future of our Church depends on faithful-
> ness to the one word of the Triune God, Jesus Christ, whom
> we are "to hear and which we are to trust and obey in life and
> in death. . . ." We are deeply concerned . . . that the commit-
> ment to "listen for God's Word in Holy Scripture" and "in our
> rich theological heritage" [declarations of a recent UCC
> General Synod] is often neglected in our Church. We view this
> indifference to Scripture and debilitating amnesia as a threat
> to the Gospel. . . . We believe we here give voice to the concerns
> of the *often-silent center* of our Church. . . . To that end we invite
> you to join us in dialogue about the meaning of that heritage
> . . . where we can *reaffirm* this faith, *reclaim* its biblical roots,
> *retrieve* its historic resources and think together about the con-
> troverted questions within our Church and the culture.[25]

Sent to 450 who had taken part since 1984 in grassroots theological colloquies begun at a UCC conference center on Cape Cod
(Craigville), four hundred pastors appeared at three regional

24. Distinctions made in Fackre, *Ecumenical Faith in Evangelical Perspective.*
25. "Confessing Christ," letter to 450 pastors, September 30, 1993, fifteen
signatories.

gatherings to express their support. Since then a national steering committee has formed, many more regional meetings have been held on controverted questions (the Re-imagining Conference, the Jesus Seminar, religious pluralism, inclusive language, the baptismal formula, etc.), eight regional centers established, a catechism project launched, publications produced including a detailed theological critique of *The New Century Hymnal: How Shall We Sing the Lord's Song?* (Pittsburgh: Pickwick Press, 1997), and Internet meetings with over seven thousand notes. The framework for these activities is a Statement of Principles in which Confessing Christ pledges to

> listen for God's Word in the Holy Scriptures of the Old and New Testaments and in our rich theological heritage. Central to the United Church of Christ, which baptizes in the name of the Father, Son and Holy Spirit, is its faith in Jesus Christ as Lord and Savior. This faith is grounded in the authority of Scripture and is expressed in the ecumenical creeds, in the confessions and covenants of our Reformation traditions, in the Preamble of its Constitution and in the prayers, worship and public witness of the Church.[26]

When the grassroots pastor movements are ranged alongside the reach toward theological integrity in many congregations, a pattern emerges: *ad fontes!* Back to the sources of who we are as confessing Christians in a culture with other regnant premises and perspectives. Their purpose is not to escape from the modern world, but to root Christian witness in and to culture in classical Christian identity, rather than be defined by society's ideologies.

The similarity between the doctrinal commitments developing in congregations and among pastors and the foci of the three ELCA ecumenical proposals is notable. In all cases, the drive is to "first principles": justification, the Trinity, the person and work of Jesus Christ, the nature, mission, ministry, and sacraments of

---

26. *Confessing Christ Statement of Principles.*

the church, the authority of Scripture and role of tradition. These are critical loci in Christian doctrine.[27] The direction of re-grounded congregations and pastors converges with the bilateral ecumenical agenda at the point of recovery of fundamental frameworks and thus the challenge to doctrinal indifferentism. Attention to the fundaments as required by the ecumenical agenda of the ELCA finds a natural ally in congregations and pastors re-interrogating the Great Tradition as a way to resist cultural captivity.

Further, the very accent on confessional identity developing in congregations and among pastors is of a piece with the Lutheran charism explored in my first lecture, the concern for sound teaching in the church. Non-Lutheran historians Mark Noll and Winfred Hudson had it right in their earlier cited comments on Lutheranism as steward of doctrinal integrity. The nature of the long discussions associated with all three proposed ELCA partnerships, and the specifics of the agreements, all highlight the importance of Christian doctrine, and as such, constitute the giving of a Lutheran gift to the ecumenical enterprise. And now the neoconfessional developments in congregations and among pastor-led movements return to these same foundations.

The case I have sought to make in my first two lectures for the giving and receiving of charisms and concerns reinforces the importance of retrieving the tradition *ecumenically*. The integrity of Christian doctrine — its wholeness — is in direct relationship to the catholicity of the church. To rephrase the Vincentian canon: Christian faith is what is held to be true always and everywhere *that the church is together*. Doctrinal authenticity is inextricable from ecclesial catholicity. The retrieval that secures Christian identity requires, therefore, a life together of the Christian community, one based on attention to shared basics the fullness of which is contingent upon the various parts of the Body bringing their charisms to one another in Corinthian mutuality.

27. On the current surge in the writing of systematics, see the issue "The Resurgence of Systematic Theology," *Interpretation* 49:3 (July 1995).

The heightened significance of congregations, their ecclesial centrality in the stewardship of Word and sacrament, and the evidences in them, and among their pastors, of doctrinal renewal suggest the importance of a local venue for a doctrinally grounded ecumenism. Congregation-wise, this could mean strengthened bonds in local communities, new relationships that give shared *faith* commitments the high visibility they are due, an enlarged circle of support for a foundational Christian identity, and the needed complementarity of charisms.

What would that life together look like in a *locale* of committed congregations and pastors involved in the 1997 decisions?

1997 Decisions and Intra-congregational Relations

As we took a frank look in *general* at the actual state of the faith in local congregations, any scenario touching local contexts for ELCA partnership must face squarely the facts of congregational and pastoral life and belief life in *particular* cases. I will confine my remarks to the decisions that propose "church fellowship" — ELCA, Episcopal, Reformed — although they may have implications also for congregations that want to explore the ecclesial fruit of the mutual lifting of Roman Catholic–Lutheran condemnations. The implementation of the churchwide agreements presupposes that the partners do, in fact, assent to the doctrinal core on which the agreements have been premised, and that the congregations involved are, in fact, communities in which the Word is rightly preached and the sacraments rightly administered. What if that is *not* the case? Given the doctrinal disarray earlier detailed, this can surely be anticipated in the local particularities of the proposed partnerships. At this point, the congregation and the pastor come center stage in ecumenical negotiations.

There are some important contextual considerations acknowledged in the past and present joint documents of those involved in the 1997 decisions. In both the Covenant of Agree-

57

ment and in the Concordat, there is no relaxation of the partners' theological standards for pastoral ministry. Exchange of ministries made possible by the agreements does not mean abandonment of patterns of belief established in a given national church and thus in a local congregation. The ELCA will still require adherence to its confessions for Episcopal priests or Reformed pastors who might seek calls, and vice versa. The same is true for "altar fellowship" and why it is so important to the ELCA, and to many of the rest of us, to be clear that its proposed partners hold to the Real Presence in the eucharist, and thus that those welcomed to a local altar/table be admonished about this assumption. While the national denominational texts and bilateral documents assert enough doctrinal commonality to warrant the exchange of clergy and common communion, *in principle*, the application, *in fact*, especially so in local congregations, brings into play the specificity of a church's doctrinal norms.

The appropriateness of this kind of contextuality, as it related to congregations in regions, was acknowledged in the 1982 agreement between the Episcopal Church and the three Lutheran Churches that had participated in the LED I and II. Leaders of regional dioceses and synods were encouraged to implement the national agreement on "Interim Sharing of the Eucharist" when

> appropriate in particular situations where the said authorities deem that local conditions are appropriate for sharing of worship jointly by congregations of the respective Churches.[28]

After the recent Righter decision in the ECUSA, and the continuing deep differences in that church, "local conditions" cannot be ignored in *when and where* an approved national Concordat can, in fact, be implemented.

---

28. "Toward Full Communion," in *"Toward Full Communion" and "Concordat of Agreement": Lutheran-Episcopal Dialogue, Series III*, ed. William A. Norgren and William G. Rusch (Minneapolis: Augsburg Fortress, 1991), 12.

The realism about the need to maintain present doctrinal standards in each church, and the reality of diversity in local circumstances, connects with a working assumption in bilateral and multilateral covenants. Assumed in many calls to "church fellowship" are two stages of decision-making: formal ratification, and subsequently what is variously described as "realization," "actualization," "reception." The distinction has to do with factors of finitude in implementing official agreements: the need for soaking time and pedagogy, and of course, the fact of inertia. However, discretionary factors are also implied. Even where denominations are purportedly connectional and disciplined, the deterioration of confidence in national structures is such that a *de facto* freedom is everywhere to be seen, as in the withholding of funds and much resistance to corporate denominational agendas and decisions. Add to this the other realities of rampant "culture-Protestantism" and the neoconfessional countermovements' response, and another kind of "church fellowship" begins to suggest itself. It might look something like this: Under the umbrella of national bilateral agreements (stage one), let there be a *measured* implementation in locales (stage two), according to the discernment of *common theological faithfulness*. When and where there is reason for "mutual affirmation" and also readiness for the sharing of charisms and thus "mutual admonition," let church fellowship go forward in fact, as well as in principle. Doctrinal circumstances therefore are the condition for the actualization of ecumenical agreements. Thus the fair question: In this local context, can congregations and regions, in good conscience, *actualize* the formally declared concord?

Such a measured discretionary second stage would coalesce with concerns of the neoconfessional movements to bring theological integrity to the foreground of church attention. Indeed it would encourage the kind of theological soul-searching that all our churches so desperately need.

Whatever the formal agreements, the fact is that bilaterals do work just this way. The Leuenberg Concord is a case in point. While there have been denominational signatories, its actual implementation has been affected by the factors of both finitude and discretion, and carried out with the same contextual caution as is here proposed.[29]

The congregation-sensitive approach to ecumenical proposals that I am exploring does honor the place of national churches and does not accede to a current "neocongregationalism" scornful of supra-parochial structures and wedded to a trendy cultural localism. Tony Campola, who as a Baptist knows the dangers of a church defined solely in terms of local autonomy, argues that denominations are carriers of the classical Christian identity regularly ignored by the booming megachurches so easily taken captive by their surrounding culture.[30] But more than pragmatically considered, the church, this Mercersburg theologian believes, is the Body of Christ, an organism born at Pentecost and sustained by the Holy Spirit corporately over time through Word, sacrament, and ministry — only fully expressing empirically what it is ontologically when having a true life together in Word, sacrament, and ministry. "Denominations," transient forms on the way to that larger communal reality, however, are serious covenantal attempts and anticipations of that hoped-for unity, and in those denominations under the glass here, are carriers of a Word, sacrament, and ministry that steward classical Christian identity. The doctrinal foci of these 1997 agreements are witness to that custodianship. Thus congregations, and their new visibility, must be seen for what they are, *cells* within the Body of Christ, not mistaken for the Body as such. Here we have given attention to *healthy* cells, worries about malignancy, and some hopes for how the healthy ones can contribute to the upbuilding of the Body of Christ.

29. On the struggle to find a life together subsequent to the declaration of concord see *Leuenberger Kirchengemeinschaft Gemeinschaft reformatorischer in Europa, Die Kirche Jesu Christi, Sacramente, Amt, Ordination*, Leuenberger Texte, Heft 1, Heft 2 (Frankfurt am Main: Verlag Otto Lembeck, 1995), English translation included.

30. Tony Campolo, *Can Mainline Churches Make a Comeback?* (Valley Forge, Penn.: Judson Press, 1995).

The Lutheran Charism in the Local Community

What would the convergences of currents of congregational and pastoral concern for sound teaching, the 1997 proposed partnerships, and the Lutheran doctrinal charism mean in a community of local congregations? I close with a scenario, intentionally "blue sky," as futurists argue the benefits of stretching the mind by considering the daring dream.

Here is a community with ELCA, Episcopal, Reformed (take your pick — RCA, UCC, PCUSA), and Roman Catholic congregations, representing the varied conversation partners. All the congregations are active in the local council of churches and their pastors in the ecumenical ministerium. These associations do many good works, but doctrinal digging and work on the foundations of sound teaching enriched by the ecumene of charisms is not one of them. The absence of such is an ecumenical invitation for building the Body of Christ in this place. Whatever else is entailed for a local ELCA congregation by any or all of these 1997 agreements, certainly in local communities and among congregations and local pastors, the ELCA congregation is a natural host to the desperately needed theological conversation about fundamental Christian teaching. If the agreements are approved in 1997, important documents of shared belief are put in place, and an enriching complementarity made possible. A local community in which the partnership congregations really did care about the things worth caring about — justification by faith, the Triune God, the Person and Work of Christ, the Real Presence of Christ in the eucharist, the witness and outreach of the church — would become the locus for rare in-depth exploration of and witness to catholic faith, with commensurate enrichment of mission in all of its senses. Indeed, the exciting and eye-opening conversation that produced the studies behind, and the documents of, 1997 could be re-lived in and among local congregations and local pastors. An ELCA congregation with the Lutheran charism could be the catalyst of this kind of local congregational life together. It would find a ready reception for that initiative in partner congregations and pastors where theological renewal now goes on apace. That kind of deep-level sharing would be the natural context and catalyst for the eucharistic hospitality and clergy interrelationships to one degree or another entailed in the various proposals. Where there is no theological seriousness and response on the part of other congregations involved in the formal 1997 agreements, no such outreach is in order and no local implementation of the overarching agreements appropriate. But I am focusing on the dream here not the nightmare, the possibility of a significant step forward toward the unity of the church in local assemblies where the Gospel is rightly preached and the sacraments rightly administered. "Mutual conversation and consolation" has a special Lutheran resonance. Why not a life together among as well as within faithful congregations? "Some speak of things that were and ask, 'Why?' I dream of things that never were, and ask, 'Why not?'"

What Are We Doing?
The Unity of the Church
and the Unity of the Churches

MICHAEL ROOT

What are we doing? And why are we doing it? Why has the Evangelical Lutheran Church in America used up so much of its theological time and energy since early in this decade debating and soon deciding the three ecumenical proposals before us: the Concordat of Agreement which would establish full communion with the Episcopal Church [hereafter, simply "the Concordat"], the Formula of Agreement which would establish full communion with three Reformed churches [hereafter, simply "the Formula"], and the Joint Declaration on the Doctrine of Justification in which the Roman Catholic Church and the Lutheran churches around the world would affirm a consensus in the basic truths of the doctrine of justification and on that basis declare that neither today condemns the other's teaching on justification [hereafter, simply "the Joint Declaration"]? What are we in fact seeking in all this? And are we seeking what we should be seeking?

In this lecture and those that follow, I want to examine three basic and simple questions: What are we doing? Should we do it? and What difference does it make? Although I will make no effort to hide the fact that I support all three of the proposals, I will not be presenting arguments directly for or against them in these lectures. That is not their function. Rather, I want to focus on the more comprehensive background questions about the nature of our ecumenical efforts. In dealing with the proposals before us, it is important both to debate their details and to keep these larger questions in mind. In the debate about the proposals so far, I fear that we have sometimes lost ourselves in the details, that we have begun to miss the forest for the trees. We need to see the proposals both in light of our total understanding of Christ, Spirit, and church and as a part of a larger process within which our decisions this summer are only one moment.

In this first lecture, I want to ask some very basic questions about the unity of the church and the communion we are seeking. In this lecture, I will remain at a rather abstract level and will say very little about the specifics of the proposals themselves. In the second lecture, I will turn more directly to the theological details of the proposals and ask about the criteria by which we might judge their acceptability. In the last lecture, which will be shorter in order to permit greater time for response and discussion, I will ask some general questions about the promises and dangers these proposals contain for American Lutheranism as it looks forward to the next century.

1. The Gift of Unity and the Pursuit of Unity

Back then to the question I began with: What are we trying to do? A simple (and, I believe, true) answer is that we are seeking to live out the unity of the church on the basis of the truth of the gospel. As soon as one makes this rather simple statement, however, a problem arises. On the one hand, there is a unity which we appear to lack. At its 1991 Assembly in Canberra, the World Council of Churches adopted a statement on "The Unity of the Church as Koinonia: Gift and Calling," *koinonia* being the Greek word usually translated as "communion." This ecumenical statement reflects a widespread consensus on the essential shape of that unity we are seeking: "The unity of the church to which we are called is a koinonia given and expressed in the common confession of the apostolic faith; a common sacramental life entered by the one baptism and celebrated together in one eucharistic fellowship; a common life in which members and ministries are mutually recognized and reconciled; and a common mission witnessing to the gospel of God's grace to all people and serving the whole of creation."[1] This unity we do not today have with many communities we nevertheless recognize as churches. We are not able to share the Eucharist with the Orthodox; Lutherans and Baptists do not have a mutual recognition of baptism; Catholics do not recognize Lutheran ordained ministries; and while we are approaching ever closer to a widely accepted joint confession of the apostolic faith, we are not yet there.[2] In America, Lutherans are themselves still separated in churches which cannot together celebrate the Lord's Supper. A unity we should display is clearly missing.

And yet, we repeatedly confess that we believe in the *one*, holy, catholic, and apostolic church. Article 7 of the Augsburg Confession states that "the one holy Christian church will be and remain forever." Oneness, unity, is essential to the church as the body of Christ and so is a characteristic the church cannot lose and still be the church. In the face of divisions in the Corinthian church, Paul asks "Has Christ been divided?" (1 Cor. 1:13) and he expects the answer to be "no." In 1 Corinthians 12, a chapter focally concerned with unity, Paul tells his addressees: "You are the body of Christ" (v. 27) and that body cannot be divided. As is said in the letter to the Ephesians, "there is one body" (4:4).

1. World Council of Churches, "The Unity of the Church as Koinonia: Gift and Calling," in *Documentary History of Faith and Order 1963-1993*, edited by Günther Gassmann. Faith and Order Paper no. 159 (Geneva: WCC Publications, 1993), 4.

2. See Faith and Order Commission, *Confessing the One Faith: An Ecumenical Explication of the Apostolic Faith as It Is Confessed in the Nicene-Constantinopolitan Creed (381)*. Faith and Order Paper no. 153 (Geneva: WCC Publications, 1991).

In addition to that unity we sense is lacking, there is then also a unity which cannot be missing if there is any church at all. In relation to this unity, all we can do is accept it or leave it; we cannot destroy it. Christ has promised that the gates of hell shall not prevail against the church (Matt. 16:18) and thus it is a matter of our faith that a united, holy, catholic, and apostolic church will always exist, not because of our effort, but as a gift of God's grace. There are the divided churches, but there is also, there *must* be, the one, undivided church.

How do we understand the relationship between the unity our churches seek and the unity we must already possess if we are churches at all? Here, I think, is where we must begin when we ask: "what are we doing?" We will rightly understand and pursue the unity we lack only when we understand it in the context of the unity which is God's prior and gracious gift in Christ and the Spirit.

2. What Unites the Church?

What in fact unites the church? What holds the church together in unity? Typically, unity is a matter of various things or persons being united by something, by some common characteristic or some common interest, or perhaps, to put it another way, united in something, some common cause, something in which persons feel themselves bound together, unified, one. What are the bonds that hold the church together? My answer will have three steps, unified in a single trajectory. Crucial for the scheme I am proposing is both the ordered distinction of these three steps and their ultimate unity. I will not be describing three unities or three forms of unity, but one unity.

2.1. Unity in Word and Sacrament

When Lutherans ask in an ecumenical context what unites or unifies the church, the discussion never goes on very long

66

without a quotation of Article 7 of the Augsburg Confession and its *satis est* clause, which I will quote in full:

> Our churches also teach that one holy church is to continue forever. The church is the assembly of saints in which the Gospel is taught purely and the sacraments are administered rightly. For the true unity of the church it is enough [*satis est*] to agree concerning the teaching of the Gospel and the administration of the sacraments. It is not necessary that human traditions or rites and ceremonies, instituted by men, should be alike everywhere. It is as Paul says, "One faith, one baptism, one God and Father of all," etc. (Eph. 4:5, 6).

We seem here to have a straightforward and simple answer to the question: What unites the church? The unity of the church is constituted by the common presence of a common event or activity: the teaching of the gospel and the administration of the sacraments. Where these activities occur, then the bonds that hold the one church together are present.

Lutherans are convinced that this statement is true. But why word and sacrament and not something else: bishops, the pope, or a common experience of being born again? The answer of the Reformation was that the church, like justification itself, is a gift of grace, not the product of human works. Crucial for the ecclesiology of the Lutheran Reformation was the conviction that justification and church go together. Justification is bound up with our being "in Christ"; I share in the righteousness of Christ and so am justified because I am in Christ and Christ in me by faith and baptism. But to be in Christ is to be in his Body, the church. Justification and the reality of the church are inseparable. If that is so, then those events that constitute and communicate justification are identical with those events that create the church and bring the individual into the church. Justification is communicated by the gospel proclaimed in word and sacrament and by nothing else. The church also, then, is constituted by the events of word and sacrament.[3]

3. On ecclesiology within the CA, I find the best study to be Bernhard

If we say that word and sacrament constitute the church, they must also constitute the church's essential characteristics: its holiness, its catholicity, its apostolicity, and its oneness, its unity. Where the word is rightly taught and the sacraments are rightly administered, there the bonds exist which unite this community with all other communities, and there the one catholic church is present. Where word and sacrament are lacking, then those bonds do not exist, and we have something else than the one church, whatever else may be present — good works, deep religious conviction, solidarity with the poor and oppressed, moving experience, or, if one likes, correctly ordained pastors or bishops. We should note how strong a doctrine of the church is implied in the statement that word and sacrament alone are truly constitutive of the church, for in saying this, the Augsburg Confession is implying the inseparability of the justification of the sinner and the coming to be of the church. This connection between justification and church is the unmovable foundation of Lutheran ecclesiology.

A foundation, however, is not yet a building. The Lutheran tendency is to stop at this point, not only to say no more, but to accuse anyone who does say more of somehow betraying the Reformation. But to stop with the statement that the church is united by common word and sacrament is unsatisfactory in a variety of ways. It is logically unsatisfactory, because it confuses two kinds of statement. It is one thing to state what are the necessary and sufficient conditions for the one church to exist. Broadly speaking, that is what Augustana 7 does. It is something

Lohse, "Die Einheit der Kirche nach der Confessio Augustana," in *Evangelium — Sakramente — Amt und die Einheit der Kirche: Die ökumenische Tragweite der Confessio Augustana*, edited by Karl Lehmann and Edmund Schlink. Dialog der Kirchen, vol. 2 (Freiburg i. B.: Herder; Göttingen: Vandenhoeck & Ruprecht, 1982). More extensive arguments in support of what is said in this lecture about the CA can be found in Michael Root, " 'Satis Est': What Do We Do When Other Churches Don't Agree?" *Dialog* 30 (1991): 314-24; Michael Root, "Conditions of Communion: Bishops, the Concordat, and the Augsburg Confession," in *Inhabiting Unity: Theological Perspectives on the Proposed Lutheran-Episcopal Concordat*, edited by Ephraim Radner and R. R. Reno (Grand Rapids: Eerdmans, 1995), 52-70.

rather different to describe what the unity is which word and sacrament creates. The unity for which word and sacrament are the necessary and sufficient conditions is far richer than just the events of word and sacrament. It is theologically unsatisfactory to stop with word and sacrament, because word and sacrament are not self-enclosed events, events that begin and end in themselves; they are events that communicate Christ and the Spirit, who are then active in the lives of individuals and in the life of the community they create. To describe the unity of the community means talking about more than word and sacrament, even if what we describe always remains dependent on and constituted by word and sacrament. To grasp the unity of the church we need to follow the trajectory taken by the work of Christ and the Spirit.

2.2. Unity in Faith as a Personal Reality

The next step in this trajectory can be seen in Melanchthon's expansion of Article 7 in the Apology. He states: "The church is not merely an association of outward ties and rites like other civic governments, however, but it is mainly [*principaliter*] an association of faith and of the Holy Spirit in men's hearts."[4] His emphasis here falls on faith as that which associates people in the church, and faith not simply in terms of its content, but as a reality in the heart.

There is of course no tension between unity as constituted by word and sacrament and unity as an internal personal reality in faith. The significance of word and sacrament is that they communicate Christ and the Spirit. Christ and the Spirit do not remain simply external to the self, but come and dwell in the believer. Faith is emphasized as that by which the believer receives Christ and the Spirit. It is this receptive role of faith that is the basis for the Lutheran insistence that we are justified by grace through faith (and not through, say, love).

4. Apol. 7.5.

Unity in word and sacrament creates unity in faith. As Luther put it: "Where there is the same gospel, there is also the same faith. . . ."[5] Because faith is dependent on word and sacrament and effected by them, when one lists what is constitutive of the church and its unity, one can speak as the Confession speaks, one can speak simply of word and sacrament. But if one wants to give a full description of what the unity of the church is, one must go on and speak of faith. Unity is not something simply external to the self. Persons are bound together in Christ's body. When pressed by the Roman Catholic *Confutation* to expand on what had been said in Augustana 7 about the church and its unity, Melanchthon took up this more internal unity:

> We are talking about true spiritual unity, without which there can be no faith in the heart nor righteousness in the heart before God. For this unity, we say, a similarity of human rites, whether universal or particular, is not necessary. The righteousness of faith is not a righteousness tied to certain traditions, as the righteousness of the law was tied to the Mosaic ceremonies, because this righteousness of the heart is something that quickens the heart. To this quickening human traditions, whether universal or particular, contribute nothing; nor are they wrought by the Holy Spirit, as are chastity, patience, the fear of God, the love of our neighbor, and the works of love.[6]

The unity constituted by word and sacrament is inseparable from the faith which receives them. It is thus a reality within the hearts and lives of believers and not simply a matter of public events.

2.3. Unity in a Common Life of Love and Mission

But can we stop here, can we say simply that the unity of the church is unity in word and sacrament and in the faith which

5. WA 7.720.
6. Apol. 7.31.

receives and is effected by word and sacrament? I believe we need to take a third step if we are to take into account the full range of what the Reformation had to say about the church's unity and, more basically, if we are to be true to the reality of faith and of the church.

In the Large Catechism, when Luther explains the phrase "I believe in the holy catholic church," he states: "This is the sum and substance of this phrase: I believe that there is on earth a little holy flock or community of pure saints under one head, Christ. It is called together by the Holy Spirit in one faith, mind, and understanding. It possesses a variety of gifts, yet is united in love without sect or schism."[7] The church has not just a common faith, but a common mind and understanding and is united in love. In the Smalcald Articles, Luther states: "The church cannot be better governed and maintained than by having all of us live under one head, Christ, and by having all the bishops equal in office (however they may differ in gifts) and diligently joined together in unity of doctrine, faith, sacraments, prayer, works of love, etc."[8] Here it is not just unity of doctrine, faith, and sacraments that joins together the leadership of the church, but also unity in prayer and works of love. The quotation I gave above, in which Luther says that the same gospel produces the same faith, reads in full: "Where there is the same gospel, there is also the same faith, same hope, same love, same spirit, and all things are truly the same."[9] Again, unity is realized in more than just a common faith, but in a more comprehensive unity of persons.

Nor are these just slips of the overproductive pen of Luther. In the Apology, Melanchthon addresses the right interpretation of Colossians 3:14, which speaks of "love, which binds everything together in perfect harmony." Against Catholic interpretations which would relate this love to justification, Melanchthon insists that Paul is "talking not about personal perfection but about fellowship in the church. He says that love is a bond and

7. LC 2.51.
8. SA 2.4.9.
9. WA 7.720.

unbroken chain linking the many members of the church with one another. . . . Paul is speaking of unity and peace in the church."[10]

What are we to make of these remarks, of which there are many more, about love as a bond of unity?[11] How are they consistent with the insistence that word, sacrament, and faith are the foundations of the unity? It is clear that for Luther, to say that we are one in faith in the heart is not to say that we are one in some isolated aspect of who we are. Faith is a fundamental and determinative orientation of the entire self. As such, faith is, as Luther said, "a living, busy, active, mighty thing."[12] Faith is not just something that happens in our heads. In faith occurs nothing less than the death of the old person and the birth of the new. As ever active, faith is lived, realized in daily life, or it simply is not. A life of faith does not just express faith, although that way of speaking is not simply wrong; it is in the life of faith that faith is realized as what it is, as a living relation to and within Christ.

The active character of faith has implications for unity in faith. We again must follow the trajectory of the work of Christ and the Spirit in the church. Christ and the Spirit come by word and sacrament and are received by faith. The unity of believers in Christ by word, sacrament, and faith is then lived out in a far-reaching unity. Again to quote Luther: "Among Christians, however, all these things are one and the same and are shared by all: the Word, faith, worship, religion, the sacraments, Christ, God, the heart, the feelings, the soul, the will."[13] Love is the typical term Luther uses to describe this wider common life. In his *Treatise on the New Testament, That Is, the Holy Mass*, he says: "Christ, in order to prepare for himself an acceptable and beloved

10. Apol. 4.232ff.
11. I made a more comprehensive study of such texts in Michael Root, "Die Einheit der Kirche in Christus, im Glauben und in der Liebe: Ekklesiologische und ökumenische Fragen," in *Der Heilige Geist: Ökumenische und reformatorische Untersuchungen*. Veröffentlichungen der Luther-Akademie, Ratzeburg, vol. 25 (Erlangen: Martin Luther Verlag, 1996), 157-68.
12. AE 35:370.
13. AE 27:91.

people which should be bound together in unity through love, abolished the whole law of Moses."[14] In a discussion of Acts 1:15-26, Luther states: "Here Christ shows incontestably that all apostles were created by him alone and are equal. This ought also to make all bishops equal and unite them, not under one authority and sovereign power as the pope's partisans deceitfully suggest to us, but in the unity of faith, baptism, love, and the Spirit, so that they would be one people, as St. Paul teaches in Eph. 4."[15]

The reference to Ephesians 4 here is helpful. This text is often in the background of statements from the Reformers on the unity of the church; it was cited at the end of Augustana 7. Ephesians 4 also grounds the unity of the church in the unity of what we receive: "There is one body and one Spirit, just as you were called to the one hope of your calling, one Lord, one faith, one baptism, one God and Father of all, who is above all and through all and in all." But this grounding does not hinder the author of Ephesians from also speaking about love as maintaining unity. The chapter begins: "I therefore . . . beg you to lead a life worthy of the calling to which you have been called, with all humility and gentleness, with patience, bearing with one another in love, making every effort to maintain the unity of the Spirit in the bond of peace" (vv. 1-3). Later in the chapter, the integration of Christ's gifts in the actual life of the church is clearly related to unity. The gifts are to work together "until all of us come to the unity of the faith and of the knowledge of the Son of God." The whole body is said to be "joined and knit together by every ligament with which it is equipped" (v. 16). Unity is in the Lord and lived out in the concrete life of the church.[16]

The total picture begins to become clear. Unity is not static,

14. AE 35:80.

15. AE 32:74.

16. A similar interpretation of the ecumenical implications of Ephesians 4 can be found in Ernst Kinder, "Basic Considerations with Reference to Article VII of the Augsburg Confession," in *The Unity of the Church: A Symposium*, Papers presented to the Commission on Theology and Liturgy of the Lutheran World Federation (Rock Island: Augustana Press, 1957), 59-73.

but occurs within a movement: the movement of Christ and the Spirit through word and sacrament, received by faith and at work in the common life and mission of the one church they create. I have used the language of trajectory to emphasize this character of movement. Both the ordering and the unity of this trajectory are important. The ordering is crucial if the evangelical character of the ecclesiology I have been presenting is to be maintained. If the existence and unity of the church are to understood as strictly a gift of grace, parallel to justification, then the proclamation of the gospel in word and sacrament and its reception in faith must be fundamental. Love must not be separated from or put in place of unity in word and sacrament or in faith. Luther was scornful of those who thought a unity in love could substitute for a unity in faith.[17] A common life in love is a third moment in the trajectory I have been describing as the living out of unity in word, sacrament, and faith.

The unity of this trajectory also must not be lost. The unity of the church is realized in the entirety of the process described by this trajectory. That unity in faith and in the life of faith follows from unity in word and sacrament does not mean that unity in faith and the life of faith are themselves dispensable. They are an aspect of what is meant by the unity of the church. Thus Luther and the Confessions can speak of love as not merely an expression of unity but as itself "a bond and unbroken chain linking the many members of the church with one another."

The most striking witness to the Reformers' sense of the unity of this trajectory can be found in the Wittenberg Articles of 1536.[18] These articles, written in negotiations between represen-

17. E.g.: "The concord of love . . . is to be subordinated to the concord of faith or of the Spirit. For if you lose this, you have lost Christ; and once you have lost Him, love will not do you any good." AE 27:107.

18. Both the Latin and German original of these articles and an English translation can be found in Gerald Bray, ed., *Documents of the English Reformation* (Minneapolis: Fortress Press, 1994), 118-61. The article cited is on pp. 142ff. Only after completing this lecture did I discover that the "bond of love" as a third *nota ecclesiae* was taken up into the Worms Book and became a controversial point in the negotiations leading up to and at Regensburg [see Georg Kret-

tatives of Henry VIII of England and the Wittenberg theologians, including Luther, are little more than a paraphrase of the Augsburg Confession. Nevertheless, without any sign of an intention to deviate from what was said at Augsburg, a small variation is introduced into the *satis est* clause of Augustana 7. The tenth of the Wittenberg Articles (On Church Order) states that it is taking up what is discussed in articles 7 and 15 of the Augsburg Confession, but makes a subtle change. It states: "It is sufficient for the maintenance of true unity that there be unity in the right teaching of the Gospel and in the correct use of the sacraments and that people live in love with one another in accordance with the Gospel, as St. Paul says: 'One faith, one baptism, etc.'" Without any sign that they are conscious of changing the content of Augustana 7, they add a common life in love to word and sacrament as what is sufficient for the true, spiritual unity of the church. For the Reformers, there was no separation of unity in word and sacrament and unity in a common life of love and mission. One leads to the other. To stop at word and sacrament is to cut short the work of Christ and the Spirit.

3. Life in Communion

I want now to use this theological picture of unity realized in a three-step trajectory to return to my earlier question: How do we understand the unity we are seeking in relation to the unity we are always already given?

The unity we are always already given is that unity constituted by word and sacrament and received in faith, that unity the Apology refers to as inseparable from faith in the heart and righteousness before God. Any community which one can de-

---

schmar, "Die Wiederentdeckung des Konzeptes der 'Apostolischen Sukzession' im Umkreis der Reformation," in *Kirche in der Schule Luthers: FS Joachim Heubach*, edited by Bengt Hägglund and Gerhard Müller (Erlangen: Martin Luther Verlag, 1995), 231-79]. These discussions require more research on my part, but I do not believe they should change my argument.

scribe as church is a realization of this one church. This unity can be described as communion in the foundational elements of salvation.

The unity we are seeking is unity in a common life of love, a common life of witness and mission with other churches. Peter Brunner, one of the most profound and most unjustly neglected Lutheran theologians of the mid-twentieth century, wrote eloquently about this move from given unity to concrete common life.

> That which is valid for the Holy Spirit drives to realize itself in concrete existence. The Spirit presses toward corporeality. Therefore, the given spiritual unity of the holy catholic church [*sancta catholica ecclesia*] works with the necessity of a *dynamis* of the Holy Spirit on the form and corporate life of the local churches [*ecclesiae*]. . . . We must recognize that the unification of the church is realized [*sich realisiert*] through an abundance of actually lived, concrete, historical, and of course, constitutionally formulated relationships and forms of expression. . . . To the continually realized and indestructible unity of the church in the spiritual body of Christ corresponds the *koinonia* of the churches of God on earth. There is also a completely legitimate plurality of churches. But all local churches [*ecclesiae*] in the whole world should stand in a concrete, actually lived, constitutionally effective *koinonia*.[19]

The communion given in word and sacrament and received in faith is to be lived out in a common life of communion or fellowship. As both a theological and a social reality, this life in communion has a structure. As a theological reality, this common life focuses on the foundations of what joins us: the one faith, bap-

---

19. Peter Brunner, "The Realization of Church Fellowship," in *The Unity of the Church*, 17-18. Translation altered. German original: Peter Brunner, "Die Einheit der Kirche und die Verwirklichung der Kirchengemeinschaft," in *Pro Ecclesia: Gesammelte Aufsätze zur dogmatischen Theologie*, vol. 1 (Berlin: Lutherisches Verlagshaus, 1962), 225-34.

tism, the Lord's Supper, and, in a subordinate way, the ministry which serves them. The focus which gives theological structure to our common life is the common witness to the one gospel and a shared participation in the sacraments. As a social reality, this common life inevitably takes on an institutional form; what Brunner referred to as a constitutionally or legally effective *koinonia*.

The various descriptions of the unity we seek found in various ecumenical documents are attempts to spell out the basic shape of this communion which lives out the communion we are given. At the beginning of this lecture I cited the description given by the World Council of Churches at its 1991 Assembly. Let me cite now the 1984 Lutheran World Federation statement on "The Unity We Seek." It follows the same trajectory I have been outlining:

> The true unity of the church, which is the unity of the body of Christ and participates in the unity of the Father, Son, and Holy Spirit, is given in and through proclamation of the gospel in Word and sacrament. [Again, true unity is this unity we are given.] This unity is expressed as a communion in the common and, at the same time, multiform confession of one and the same apostolic faith. It is a communion in holy baptism and in the eucharistic meal, a communion in which the ministries exercised are recognized by all as expressions of the ministry instituted by Christ in his church. . . . It is a committed fellowship, able to make common decisions and to act in common.[20]

There is today a widespread ecumenical agreement on the essential elements of life in communion: a common confession of the faith (not just a recognition that we each confess the faith but the possibility of stating it together); a mutual recognition of baptism; the possibility of celebrating the Lord's Supper together; mutual

---

20. Lutheran World Federation, Seventh Assembly, "The Unity We Seek," Assembly statement in *Budapest 1984: In Christ — Hope for the World,* Proceedings of the Seventh Assembly, Lutheran World Federation. LWF Report, no. 19 (Geneva, 1985), 175.

recognition of ordained ministries, implying a mutual availability of clergy; and whatever common structures of action and decision making are necessary to carry out common mission. This listing of elements is not yet a concrete model of unity; much is still left open. Yet it does provide, I believe, a basic picture of what it is we are seeking. In 1991, the ELCA officially adopted a very similar picture of the communion we seek in its ecumenical policy statement.[21]

As I noted at the beginning of this lecture, we lack this unity of a common life in worship and mission with many other bodies we have come to recognize as also churches of Jesus Christ. What is the significance of this lack of unity? On the one hand, it is true that this common life is not in a strict sense necessary to the true, spiritual unity of the church. There may be historical occasions when many aspects of this common life are made impossible. Obviously enough, when many ethnic German Lutherans in the Soviet Union were exiled to central Asia under Stalin and cut off from the world for decades, their churches could not enjoy a common life in communion with other churches. This oppression could not destroy, however, their essential unity with the church of Christ. As long as they gathered around the gospel, there the one church of Christ was present, there they were one with the saints of all times and places. This is one aspect of what it means to say that the gates of hell will not prevail against Christ's church.

On the other hand, however, this common life in communion is not dispensable in the sense that we are free to dispense with it when it does not suit us. Because this common life in communion is not strictly necessary in an unconditional sense does not mean that it may not be mandatory in many situations. When such a common life is possible, it is a practical denial of our unity in Christ to reject it. All communities which are churches are one. Not to live out that oneness is then to live in self-contradiction. Our present situation, in which we find that

21. *Ecumenism: The Vision of the ELCA*, English text with Spanish, German, and French translations (Minneapolis: Augsburg, 1994).

we cannot deny that other communities are in fact realizations of the one church of Jesus Christ and yet we do not live a common life in communion with them, is precisely one of self-contradiction. This self-contradiction is most pointed when we recognize that we and others both celebrate the one Supper of the Lord and yet we cannot celebrate it together. Here a failure to live out our common relation to the Lord must place a question mark next to the assertion that we are truly one.

Much emphasis has been put on the possibilities for mission that the proposals before us will (or will not) open. I would not deny the importance of such matters. Nevertheless, I believe we should seek to establish such relations of communion with other churches even if such possibilities of common mission appeared meager. Or rather, better put, what mission is centrally about is witness, and one aspect of our witness is to the unity and reconciliation we have been given in Christ. Living out our unity is not just a means for carrying out our call; it is an aspect of the call itself. If the descriptions of the nature of a life in communion made in texts like the LWF statement on "The Unity We Seek" or the ELCA Ecumenical Policy Statement are correct, then we are obliged to seek such a communion with other bodies we recognize as churches. As the international Anglican–Roman Catholic dialogue put it: "Those who have received the same word of God and have been baptized in the same Spirit cannot, without disobedience, acquiesce in a state of separation."[22]

This obligation does not automatically mean that we should adopt the proposals before us. There can be good arguments for rejecting specific proposals. Perhaps there are good arguments against the proposals we are now considering. In the next lecture I will address the question of the criteria I think we need to apply in making ecumenical decisions. If what I have said in this lecture

22. Anglican–Roman Catholic International Commission, "Final Report," in *Growth in Agreement: Reports and Agreed Statements of Ecumenical Conversations on a World Level*, edited by Harding Meyer and Lukas Vischer. Faith and Order Paper no. 108 (New York: Paulist Press; Geneva: World Council of Churches, 1984), Introduction, par. 9.

is true, however, then our present situation of division is deeply unsatisfactory. When we are able to recognize the one church of Jesus Christ in another community, we should have a bias in favor of proposals that will open the way to life in communion with such a body. In other words, the burden of proof rests on rejecting such proposals, not on accepting them.

4. Conclusion

In this lecture, I have remained rather abstract. I have tried to set a very general background for our ecumenical discussions, derived from basic considerations about the church and its unity. The unity of the church is, I believe, given in the proclamation of the gospel in word and sacrament, received in faith, and lived out in the common life of love and witness. In the various descriptions of communion, fellowship, or visible unity to be found in recent ecumenical documents, we have attempts to spell out more concretely what shape this common life should take.

I began with the question: What are we trying to do? We are not trying by our efforts to create the unity of Christ's church. That unity is a gift of grace inseparable from our unity with the Risen Christ himself. Rather, we are seeking to live out that unity in a way appropriate both to the gospel and to our time and conditions. What we must decide is whether the Formula, the Concordat, and the Joint Declaration are in fact true to the gospel and true to our time. These will be the subjects for my second and third lectures.

Should We Do It?
The Question of Criteria

MICHAEL ROOT

In my first lecture, I sought to provide a framework for understanding what we are trying to do ecumenically. We are not
seeking to create the unity of the church; we are seeking to live
out the unity we are given in word and sacrament in a comprehensive life in communion with other churches with which we
are one in Christ. Ecumenical proposals, such as those before us,
are proposals for how this might be done.

I argued that the nature of unity as already given means
that when we are able to recognize another body as church, we
should be prejudiced in favor of communion with them, if such
is possible. Because we are already one, we are called to live out
that unity. The burden of proof is on rejecting, not on accepting,
a proposal for communion with a community we recognize as a
church.

Experience shows, however, that the acceptability of ecumenical proposals is rarely self-evident. Because ecumenical relations touch our sense of identity, of who we are, ecumenical
proposals tend to call forth passionate debate. We can make this
debate more rational if we have some clear sense of the criteria
by which we might decide on the acceptability of ecumenical
proposals.

1. Criteria for Judging Ecumenical Proposals

We undoubtedly need a variety of criteria. Some criteria will be practical: how much can a particular church take on in a particular period of time; how should the growth of a particular relation be paced; how do we preserve a consistency in our relations in various directions; how do we not foreclose future ecumenical possibilities? Lutherans, however, have notoriously stressed more conceptual and immediately theological criteria. If the church is constituted by the right teaching of the gospel and administration of the sacraments, then an unconditional necessity for fellowship is a shared understanding of what the gospel is and how it is embodied in preaching and the sacraments. With greater consistency than perhaps any other Christian tradition, Lutherans have focused their ecumenical efforts on doctrinal dialogues as the most important precondition for entering life in communion. The most important criterion of the acceptability of ecumenical proposals has been said to be agreement on the gospel proclaimed in word and sacrament. It is on this theological criterion that I want to focus in this lecture, with explicit reference to the proposals before us.

To say that a condition of communion is agreement on the gospel in word and sacrament is deceptively simple. Problems arise as soon as one asks: what sort of agreement? Agreement on the fundamentals, on the "chief parts of Christian doctrine," as the Formula of Concord says at one point?[1] Or agreement on "doctrine and all its articles," as the Formula also says?[2] American Lutherans have been and the ELCA and the Missouri Synod still are divided on the question of the sort of agreement presupposed by church fellowship.

A bit of reflection should make clear that the consensus we seek in ecumenical dialogues must not be a consensus on every theological detail. We are seeking only that consensus needed for the common life to which we are called. This life does not require

1. Cp. SD, Summary Formulation, 15.
2. Cp. Ep. 10.7.

agreement on every disputed point. There have always been what one might describe as school differences in the church (and my experience of seminaries is that there are usually differences within schools). Harding Meyer has helpfully described the sort of agreement we are ecumenically seeking as an internally differentiated consensus.[3] In relation to each topic, we must ask, on what aspects of this topic do we need agreement. The differentiation is not between topics requiring agreement and those not; the differentiation is in relation to each topic. It is internal to each topic. Even if the doctrine of justification is the article by which the church stands and falls, we do not need to agree on every aspect of justification in order to say we are in fact preaching the same gospel rightly.

But how do we know when we have reached an adequate consensus? In an earlier essay I have proposed what one might call a pragmatic ecclesiological criterion, describing it in what I hope to be a confessionally neutral way, that is, in a way that is not itself specifically Lutheran.[4] One must not forget that ecumenical agreement is not about the relation between two abstract theological systems (as if modern American denominations could be identified with theological systems), but about the possible relation between two churches. The question is: Can we regularly and in a comprehensive range of situations carry out together with another church those activities we believe are essential to the identity of the church as church without violating our understanding of the identity of the church? If we can, then there are no church-dividing differences between us; or better put, no communion-hindering differences. Each party to an ecumenical proposal must ask itself this question. I will repeat the question: Can we carry out together with another church regularly and in a comprehensive range of situations those activities

3. Harding Meyer, "Ecumenical Consensus: Our Quest for and the Emerging Structures of Consensus," *Gregorianum* 77 (1996): 213-25.

4. Michael Root, "Identity and Difference: The Ecumenical Problem," in *Theology and Dialogue: Essays in Conversation with George Lindbeck*, edited by Bruce Marshall (Notre Dame: University of Notre Dame Press, 1990).

we believe are essential to the identity of the church as church without violating our understanding of the identity of the church? Let me elaborate.

The decisive question about any proposal should be: Will it structure a relation within which two or more churches can carry out a common life in communion so that they might regularly, not just on special occasions, and in a comprehensive range of situations, not just in certain limited cases of chaplaincies or ecumenical conferences, carry out together whatever each views as essential to the identity of the church as church without either side violating its own understanding of the identity of the church? If we believe that what is crucial to the identity of the church is the preaching of the true gospel and the evangelical administration of the sacraments, the question is whether we can carry out these activities with another church on a regular basis in a way that accords with our understanding of the fundamental integrity of these activities. In short: Can we together do everything essential to a common life in Christ? Can we regularly hear Reformed or Anglican preaching as the preaching of the gospel without protest? Can we participate in a Reformed or Anglican Eucharist on a regular basis without violation of conscience? Can we together order the ministries which serve the Word? Can we regularly carry out the mission of the church within the structure of the proposed relation without compromising that mission? If the answer to such questions is yes, then I believe we are obligated to accept the proposal for communion. If one feels that a proposal is unacceptable, then one should be able to specify at what point the proposal in question proposes a common activity that cannot be so carried out without violation of the church's identity as church.

My description of this practice-oriented criterion has been very brief and perhaps rather opaque. I hope it will become clearer as I proceed. In this lecture, I will ask how this criterion applies to the traditional doctrinal issues involved in the three proposals before us. My primary goal is to clarify what the precise issue is in each proposal. In each case, I want to state as clearly as possible what the decision before us is. In the final lecture, I want to ask the far more difficult question about the whole enterprise of doctrinal agreement as a basis for church fellowship among contemporary American Protestant denominations.

2. Justification, Presence, Episcopacy: The Dogmatic Questions in the Three Proposals

The three proposals before us are textbook examples of internally differentiated consensus. None of the proposals claims that all traditional disagreements have now been eliminated. Each seeks to outline a central framework of theological agreement, within which the remaining disagreements can be seen as not blocking communion. The central doctrinal question in relation to each is whether in fact the remaining disagreement is communion-hindering or church-dividing — that is, whether the remaining differences mean that we cannot lead a common life in communion without violating what we believe to be the church's essential identity. I will analyze each proposal in turn.

2.1. *Justification and the Joint Declaration*

Let me begin with in some ways the simplest example, but in others, the most difficult: the Joint Declaration on the Doctrine of Justification involving the churches of the Lutheran World Federation and the Roman Catholic Church.[5] On the basis of the U.S. Lutheran-Catholic dialogue on justification and especially the German Lutheran-Reformed-United/Roman Catholic discussion on the doctrinal condemnations of the sixteenth century, the LWF and the Vatican over the last four years have been working toward a common declaration that would declare a

5. All references will be to paragraph numbers and will be included within the text. For the sake of full disclosure, I should say that I was a member of the committee that carried out the last two revisions of the Joint Declaration.

85

"consensus on the basic truths of the doctrine of justification" (#40) and also, on the basis of this consensus, declare that the various Reformation-era condemnations of each other's teaching on justification do not today apply (#41). The Joint Declaration itself is meant to summarize and focus the wide-ranging discussion of justification in the various Lutheran-Catholic dialogues. Attached to the Joint Declaration is an appendix of sources, quotations from the various dialogues keyed to the various sections of the Joint Declaration.

The Joint Declaration claims to represent an internally differentiated consensus in just the sense I earlier described. Both for the doctrine of justification as a whole and for a series of individual controversial points, the Joint Declaration spells out a framework of agreement followed by a presentation of the differing ways each side then goes on to elaborate the details of a specific issue. Sometimes the differences are only of emphasis; sometimes they are straightforward disagreements. In either case, the claim is that our present agreement about the doctrine of justification itself and its place within the whole of Christian teaching is such that this doctrine no longer need block communion between Lutherans and Catholics.

Unlike the Reformed and Episcopal proposals, the Joint Declaration will not lead immediately to fellowship. This difference makes the task of evaluation in some ways simpler; practical issues do not intrude in the same way. It also makes that task more difficult, or at least more abstract. The pragmatic criterion I have proposed lacks a point of contact if pragmatic consequences do not follow. We must then ask a somewhat hypothetical question: Viewed in abstraction from other, outstanding differences, would the remaining disagreements on justification prove an obstacle to communion? About each remaining disagreement, a Lutheran must ask, what might be evangelically at stake here? Does this or that aspect of the Roman Catholic teaching on justification which we do not share distort the actual communication of the gospel as saving truth and justifying promise?

Let me highlight two aspects of the Joint Declaration as

examples of the sort of question we must ask. First, an important but slippery difference between Lutherans and Catholics has been the role of the doctrine of justification within the totality of the church's teaching and practice. In what sense is the doctrine of justification the center of the Christian message which can then be used as a criterion to judge all that the church says and does? A paragraph of the Joint Declaration addresses this question. I will quote it at length:

> The doctrine of justification . . . is more than just one part of Christian doctrine. It stands in an essential relation to all truths of faith, which are to be seen as internally related to each other. It is an indispensable criterion which constantly serves to orient all the teaching and practice of our churches to Christ. When Lutherans emphasize the unique significance of this criterion, they do not deny the interrelation and significance of all truths of faith. When Catholics see themselves as bound by several criteria, they do not deny the special function of the message of justification. Lutherans and Catholics share the goal of confessing Christ, who is to be trusted above all things as the one Mediator (1 Tim. 2:5-6) through whom God in the Holy Spirit gives himself and pours out his renewing gifts. [#18]

This paragraph adopts a specific ecumenical strategy. It elaborates a common conviction, that the doctrine of justification is a necessary criterion of the church's teaching and practice, and then seeks to allay the anxieties each has about the other's more specific teaching. When Catholics see other doctrines as also playing a role as criterion, they are not denying the special role of the doctrine of justification; when Lutherans stress the unique role of this doctrine, they are not isolating it from its interrelation with other teachings of the church.

If one believes that this agreement is insufficient, one should be able to say what communion-hindering distortion of the gospel would follow from the continuing disagreement. (It should be noted that the Joint Declaration addresses only the status of the doctrine of justification as criterion, not its concrete application to areas of teaching and practice such as authority or ministry.)[6]

A second example of differentiated consensus in the Joint Declaration is the topic which proved the most difficult in the writing of the text, the continuing sinfulness of the justified person. The text notes that Lutherans and Catholics agree, first, that in baptism the person is truly justified and united with Christ; second, that the justified person continues to have desires which stand in objective contradiction to God and with which the Christian must struggle; third, that these desires do not themselves separate the faithful person from Christ; and fourth, that the justified person remains dependent on forgiving grace throughout his or her life. Lutherans, however, go on to say that this internal struggle means that the justified person does not love God with an undivided mind and heart. As a result, this person, even while justified, must still be called a sinner and, since the judgment of God relates to the person as a whole, a sinner as a whole. The contradiction to God within the self must thus itself be called sin. Catholics, however, insist that baptism, if it truly justifies, regenerates, and unites with God, must remove anything that would itself lead to damnation. In addition, they define the word "sin" so that it is strictly applicable only to that which in fact leads to damnation. Catholic doctrine thus denies that the tendencies and desires of the old person can rightly be called sin as long as the person remains joined to Christ.

When the question is raised, can the God-opposing desires of the justified person rightly be called sin, Lutherans and Catholics give directly contradictory answers. While this difference is partly attributable to differing definitions of the word "sin," it also points to broader differences in theological anthropology.

6. For a survey that shows that Lutherans and Catholics have widely agreed that the doctrine of justification is such a criterion, but not on its concrete application, see Harding Meyer, "The Text 'The Justification of the Sinner' in the Context of Previous Ecumenical Dialogues on Justification," in *Justification by Faith: Do the Sixteenth Century Condemnations Still Apply?* edited by Karl Lehmann, translated by Michael Root and William G. Rusch (New York: Continuum, 1997), 69-97.

The Joint Declaration claims that in light of the agreement I have outlined, this disagreement need not itself block communion. If one were to disagree with this conclusion, one would need to show how the remaining disagreement leads to a fundamental distortion of the proclamation of the gospel.

The question we must ask ourselves in relation to the Joint Declaration is then: Do the remaining disagreements constitute an obstacle to a common proclamation of the gospel? The claim of the Joint Declaration is that they do not.

2.2. Real Presence and the Formula of Agreement

Unlike the Joint Declaration, the Formula of Agreement with the Reformed churches and the Concordat of Agreement with the Episcopal Church both would establish full communion among the churches involved. Evaluation is thus more complex, since a variety of practical factors must be taken into account. While complicating matters, however, this practical dimension also provides a context within which one can apply the pragmatic criterion to which I have been referring in a more realistic way.

As proposals for fellowship, both the Concordat and the Formula presuppose a comprehensive agreement in the gospel. Both texts have been modified in recent months to strengthen their claims for a general doctrinal agreement. So far, when the debate over the Formula and the Concordat has addressed *what* the churches hold (rather than *how* they hold it), the debate has not centered around the adequacy of the content of this general agreement in the gospel. Rather, it has tended to focus on certain specific and relatively traditional controversial issues. In the next lecture, I want to return to the question of how the churches hold their doctrine. In this lecture, I will look at the specific issues in each proposal that have elicited debate.

In this lecture, I am only looking at the more traditional doctrinal questions. Between the Lutheran and Reformed traditions, various issues have been disputed and at times have been held to be church-dividing: the place of the law in the Christian life, the nature of the unity of Christ's two natures, the relation between divine grace and human response, the relation between God's intent to save and the non-salvation of the lost, the possibility of truly accepting and then losing grace, the New Testament basis of a particular church order. On some of these issues, the positions of the churches have changed and so the disputes have become moot; some other remaining differences, for example in relation to how to do social ethics, are rarely today asserted to be an obstacle to fellowship. The difficult issue has remained the Lord's Supper.

A long series of Lutheran-Reformed dialogues has made clear that the official teaching of the Reformed churches rejects a Zwinglian reading of the Supper as a memorial meal at which the primary actor is the congregation which remembers. The remaining difficulty has rather centered around the interrelation among three things: the presence of Christ in his body and blood, the elements of bread and wine, and the reception by the communicant. Historically, the Reformed have usually held that the difference over this interrelation is not in itself a hindrance to communion. The Lutherans have been the ones who have seen here a problem that must be settled. We must again ask: What about the Reformed position might lead one to think that a unity in the Lord's Supper would be impossible without compromising what we understand to be the evangelical heart of the celebration? I believe we must here both take seriously the concerns of our Lutheran forebears, which cannot be reduced to mere hairsplitting over the mode of Christ's presence, and also take seriously the solution to the problem picked up by the Formula from the European Leuenberg Agreement among Lutheran, Reformed, and United churches.

In a few minutes, I can only in a very summary way address the complex issue of the presence of Christ in the sacrament. I would argue, however, that the decisive evangelical issue is not directly the relation between Christ's body and blood and the eucharistic elements. Rather, the crucial issue is the dependability of the external word. Can I receive the bread and wine with the assurance that, regardless of my internal state, I am receiving the saving body and blood of Christ? An understanding of the presence of Christ that undermines the possibility of looking away from one's own state and looking toward the promised presence is deeply problematic, not because it might make some metaphysical mistake about the mode of presence, but because it undermines the communicant's confidence in the external word of the sacrament.

Herein lies the Lutheran worry over the classical Reformed doctrine. In the interest of rejecting certain late medieval practices (which the Lutherans also wished to reject) and of preserving what they understood to be the integrity of the human nature of the risen Christ, the Reformed came to an understanding of the nature of the presence of Christ in the Supper which denied (or seemed to deny) that those who received without true faith had in fact received Christ. The problem can be seen in what is, in this respect, a good Reformed document, the Anglican Thirty-Nine Articles, number 29 of which bears the title: "Of the Wicked, which eat not the Body of Christ in the use of the Lord's Supper." If I must have true faith to receive Christ, then the call to look away from my own internal state and concentrate on the promise of Christ's presence would seem to be endangered.

Like the Wittenberg Concord of 1536, which settled the differences over the Supper between the Lutherans and the Upper German cities, including my present home city of Strasbourg,[7] the 1973 Leuenberg Agreement in Europe represented a breakthrough not so much in its definition of the relation between Christ and the elements as in its focus on the question of who receives Christ.[8] The relation between Christ's

---

7. The original Latin of the Wittenberg Concord is in CR III, cc.75ff; an English translation can be found in Henry E. Jacobs, *Historical Introduction, Appendixes and Indexes*, vol. 2 of *The Book of Concord, or the Symbolical Books of the Evangelical Lutheran Church* (Philadelphia: United Lutheran Publication House, 1908), 283-90.

8. The Leuenberg Agreement can be found in James E. Andrews and Joseph A. Burgess, eds., *An Invitation to Action: A Study of Ministry, Sacraments, and Recognition*, The Lutheran-Reformed Dialogue Series III, 1981-1983 (Philadelphia: Fortress Press, 1984), 61-73. Paragraph references will be given in the text.

body and blood and the elements is described in the Agreement simply by means of the preposition "with." More decisively, it affirms, first, that Christ "gives himself unreservedly to all who receive the bread and wine; faith receives the Lord's Supper for salvation, unfaith for judgment" (#18) and second, that "we cannot separate communion with Jesus Christ in his body and blood from the act of eating and drinking" (#19). These statements are quoted and affirmed in the Formula.[9] The relation between Christ and the elements is addressed only obliquely; the emphasis falls on the assurance that to receive the elements is always also to receive Christ. In this way, the Lutheran concern is addressed.

The traditional dogmatic question we must decide in judging the Formula is whether this agreement suffices. If one accepts that the evangelical concern in the dispute with the Reformed over the Supper is as I earlier described it, a concern for the dependability of the external word, then this agreement should suffice. If one believes that a communion-hindering difference still exists in this area, then, again, one needs to state how the remaining difference blocks a common eucharistic life, how it makes a common eucharistic life impossible without compromising the gospel.

2.3. Episcopacy and the Concordat of Agreement

Even more than Lutheran-Reformed dialogue, Lutheran-Anglican dialogue in the twentieth century has focused on a single topic as potentially blocking communion: episcopacy. On the first day of the first Lutheran-Anglican dialogue of this century, the Anglican-Swedish dialogue of 1909, one of the Swedish participants, Bishop H. W. Tottie, recommended moving immediately

9. Evangelical Lutheran Church in America, *Lutheran-Episcopal and Lutheran-Reformed Ecumenical Proposals*, Documents for Action by the 1997 Churchwide Assembly (Chicago: Evangelical Lutheran Church in America, 1996), 21. The citation is at the end of the section "Differing Emphases: The Condemnations."

to the question of episcopacy, since that is where the difficult issue lay.[10] The difficulty, of course, lies not in episcopacy itself; the majority of Lutherans in the world today are members of churches within which some ministers are titled "bishop." Rather the problem lies most immediately in the significance of the presence or absence of the office of bishop structured and understood in a certain way.

Various national and international Anglican-Lutheran dialogues have shown that Anglicans and Lutherans affirm much in common about ministry in the church. Anglicans and Lutheran agree that the office of ministry is divinely instituted and thus the church is not free to do away with it. Anglicans and Lutherans agree extensively about the primary tasks of this office. The difficult issue between Anglicans and Lutherans has been the ministry of oversight and thus the nature and importance of episcopacy.

Again, on this issue the Concordat represents an internally differentiated consensus. The Concordat claims an agreement that episcopacy in a succession of laying on of hands can be a desirable sign but not a guarantee of the unity and continuity of the church. In the period of intense negotiations between 1530 and 1541 over a possible settlement of the impending schism of the Western church, the Saxon Lutherans consistently expressed a willingness to accept the traditional episcopal structure for the sake of unity if the Catholic bishops would permit the preaching of the gospel and the reform of church practice along the lines indicated in Part II of the Augsburg Confession. This willingness is confessionally enshrined in the Augustana, the Apology, and the Smalcald Articles and thus has some sort of authoritative status for contemporary Lutherans. If the Concordat is adopted, episcopacy in succession would move from being a theoretical

---

10. The Church of England and the Church of Sweden, *Report of the Commission appointed by the Archbishop of Canterbury in Pursuance of Resolution 74 of the Lambeth Conference of 1908 on the Relation of the Anglican Communion to the Church of Sweaen, with Three Appendices* (London: Mowbray; Milwaukee: Young Churcnman, 1911), 7.

possibility for the ELCA to being a reality in the process of enactment. Thus, unlike the Joint Declaration and the Formula, the Concordat asks the ELCA to make certain changes for the sake of unity, unity not just with the Episcopal Church but also possibly with other churches in the future. It is thus not surprising that among the proposals before us, the Concordat has elicited the most vehement debate. One question we must ask ourselves is whether the total package of the Concordat, both its movement toward unity and the changes it represents, is desirable.

As a differentiated consensus, however, the Concordat does not remove all differences, and the most vehement theological debate about the Concordat has centered on implications of the remaining difference in the relative importance Anglicans and Lutherans ascribe to episcopacy in succession. At this point, I think we must very carefully describe this difference and the possible problems it creates. Perhaps this difference represents a reason to reject the Concordat, but we should be clear about what we are rejecting.[11]

The remaining difference seems to me the following: For Anglicans, the office of bishop in succession as a sign of unity has such an importance that they will only enter a relation of full communion with churches which are at least moving toward the common possession of this office. Lutherans, however, even those Lutherans in churches with an episcopacy in succession, do not place such an importance on episcopacy. The Swedish and Finnish Lutheran churches, the other Nordic churches which have adopted the Porvoo Common Statement and thus have adopted a succession of episcopal consecrations as a sign of unity and continuity, the various Asian, African, and Latin American churches with an episcopacy in succession are all in full altar and

11. My analysis here is made in greater detail and with an argument that the conditionality implied within the Concordat is acceptable to Lutherans in Michael Root, "Conditions of Communion: Bishops, the Concordat, and the Augsburg Confession," in *Inhabiting Unity: Theological Perspectives on the Proposed Lutheran-Episcopal Concordat*, edited by Ephraim Radner and R. R. Reno (Grand Rapids: Eerdmans, 1995), 52-70.

pulpit fellowship with the non-episcopal Lutheran churches. The Concordat does not eliminate this difference: The Episcopal church will remain in fellowship only with churches with a commitment to entering episcopal succession; the ELCA will remain in fellowship with the non-episcopal churches of the LWF and will be in communion with the non-episcopal Reformed churches if it adopts the Formula.

Why might one think that this difference makes the Concordat unacceptable, since it does not require the ELCA to take up the Episcopal Church's understanding of episcopacy? The problem raised by the Dissenting Report to the Concordat centers on the question: Does the Episcopal Church in the Concordat make episcopacy in succession a condition of communion, i.e., something that must be present for communion to be established? If so, then accepting the Concordat would involve accepting that something other than word and sacrament is necessary for the unity of the church and thus denying the basic ecclesiology of the Augsburg Confession I cited in my previous lecture. Any adequate discussion of the problem raised by this question must distinguish differing ways one might see episcopal succession as a "condition of communion."

First, one might see episcopal succession as necessary for communion because one thought that ordination by a bishop in succession was a condition for the valid or authentic exercise of the office of ministry. Someone ordained by anyone other than a bishop in succession might then be doing very important work, but they would not be carrying out the divinely instituted office of ministry. If one held such a belief, then one could recognize and accept the ministry of persons ordained in another church only if the ministers of that church were ordained by bishops in succession.

Such a belief would make episcopal succession an essential element in the strict sense of the divinely instituted office of ministry. It would seem to make episcopal succession necessary for unity at the very first step in the trajectory I discussed in my earlier lecture, unity in the right preaching of the word and celebration of the sacraments. Lutherans have found this sort of conditionality deeply problematic. It would seem to undercut the decisive connection between church and justification by grace I elaborated in the previous lecture; it would seem to make something beyond the gospel proclaimed in word and sacrament necessary as foundational for the church and thus also necessary for salvation. When Lutherans have discussed and rejected episcopal succession as a condition of communion they have usually been thinking of this sort of conditionality.

The Concordat clearly does not imply, however, this sort of conditionality. Central to the Concordat is the proposal that the two churches will recognize and accept each other's ordained ministries from the outset, without anything that might be interpreted as a new ordination. Any Anglican who really believed that ordination by a bishop in succession is strictly essential to the divinely instituted office of ministry could not consistently accept the Concordat.

As my description of the difference that remains even if the Concordat is adopted should make clear, however, I think one must admit that there is a second sense in which for the Episcopal Church and all Anglican churches, episcopal succession is a sort of condition of communion, at least as something toward which the churches in communion are moving. Such a condition does not concern unity at the first step in the trajectory I outlined, unity in the true preaching of word and celebration of the sacraments, but can only relate to unity at the third step, unity in the actual living out of communion in a common life. Two things need to be said about this conditionality.

First, the Concordat in no way implies that the ELCA would now or at any time in the future adopt the policy of the Episcopal Church. The ELCA is free to remain in full communion with non-episcopal churches.

Second, the reasons one might have for such a conditionality should be noted. One possible reason, the reason put forward by one of the most important Anglican ecumenical documents, the Lambeth Appeal of 1920, is a belief that the reunion of Christendom will not occur without a ministry recognized by all the churches and that only a ministry in episcopal succession stands any chance of being universally recognized.[12] For such an argument, the reason for insisting on a willingness to enter episcopal succession as part of the total set of relations which go to make up communion would not be an insistence that episcopal succession was essential to a valid ordained ministry. The insistence would rather have to do with the contextual necessities of a movement toward a common life which could include not only Anglicans and Lutherans, but also, at some time in the future, also the two-thirds of the Christians in the world who belong to the Catholic and Orthodox churches.

I would not argue that the position of the 1920 Lambeth Appeal is the only possible reason an Anglican might have for taking up the Anglican position implied in the Concordat. What seems to me clear, however, is that the Anglican position implied within the Concordat is not the position Lutherans have usually seen as blocking communion; it does not view succession as strictly necessary for a true ministry of word and sacrament. It thus does not view succession as necessary for the true unity of the church referred to in Augustana 7. The Anglican position is one that sees some structures as having evolved within the common life in communion in such a way that, while they are not necessary to salvation and thus not strictly necessary for the existence and unity of the church, they are gifts which they strongly wish to preserve, which they even might feel themselves obliged to preserve. Anglicans here can be seen as challenging the Lutheran tendency to classify all aspects of the church into two and only two categories: the absolutely essential and the strictly adiaphoral. The Anglican position, especially as it has evolved in recent ecumenical and official statements, implies a third category: the nonessential but nevertheless normally normative. The question before us then is whether this more limited, contextual form of conditionality is so radically unacceptable that it forces us to reject the Concordat. I have argued elsewhere that

12. Lambeth Conference 1920, "An Appeal to All Christian People," in *The Six Lambeth Conferences: 1867-1920,* edited by Randall Davidson (London: SPCK, 1928), 28.

MICHAEL ROOT

I believe this conditionality is not itself grounds for rejecting the Concordat, but that is an argument for another day. What I want to stress here is the analytical point about what the Concordat actually says and implies. It is this that we should accept or reject.

I have focused on the conditionality question because that is where the published Dissent and a significant amount of debate have focused. Of course, even if this issue is settled, there remains the question whether the changes for which the Concordat calls are changes we believe are either in themselves good ideas or at least acceptable in the pursuit of unity. The Concordat does imply small but not insignificant shifts in our understanding of the relation between episcopacy and other forms of the one pastoral office and in our understanding of succession as a sign but not guarantee of unity and continuity in mission. If one believes that these changes are in themselves desirable, as I do, they of course form no obstacle to accepting the Concordat. If one does not find them desirable, then one must make a judgment whether their undesirability is outweighed by the contribution the Concordat would make to the advancement of the unity of the church. Such a judgment is a matter of discernment, of weighing various considerations against one another. Such judgments are notoriously difficult.

The task I have set myself in this lecture has been a limited one: to outline an admittedly abstract criterion for assessing ecumenical proposals and then to apply that to the way the proposals before us handle the traditional doctrinal issues that have been seen as church-dividing. These issues have received much attention so far in the debate, but they are not the only issues. I will broaden my perspective a bit in the third and final lecture.

What Difference Does It Make? The Ecumenical Decisions and the Future of American Lutheranism

MICHAEL ROOT

In the first of these lectures, I sought to present a general picture of what we are seeking ecumenically. In the second lecture, I discussed the nature of an ecumenical agreement as an internally differentiated consensus, a consensus on those aspects of a topic on which we need to agree to live in communion. This understanding of consensus was closely tied to the criterion I presented to judge ecumenical proposals: Will a proposal allow the churches regularly and in a comprehensive range of situations to carry out together all those activities they believe are essential to the identity of the church as church without violating their understanding of the identity of the church? Within the lecture, I sought to apply that criterion to the proposals before us at least to the extent that might allow us better to see how they handle the traditional doctrinal issues that have been seen as church-dividing.

In the course of introducing the proposed criterion, however, I remarked that ecumenical proposals are always proposals for communion between actual churches, not between theological systems. If that passing remark is taken seriously, it represents a challenge to what I then did in the remainder of the lecture. I proceeded the way we often proceed in ecumenical discussions. Not only did I limit myself to the traditional doctrinal issues, I spoke as if the churches had clearly defined doctrinal positions which could be plausibly treated as *the* teaching of the church in question. I thus focused on the wording of various texts and confessions, following a regularly repeated axiom of ecumenical method, that one deals with the official teaching of churches, not with anecdotal evidence of what this pastor or that bishop may have said or done.

But if communion is a relation between really existing churches, then is such an approach adequate? Must we ask not only what the churches hold, but how they hold it? The ELCA, the Roman Catholic Church, the Episcopal Church, and the United Church of Christ may all formally subscribe to the classical christological affirmations of Nicea and Chalcedon, but what is the lived reality of that formal affirmation? What does the formal affirmation tell us about what we will in fact encounter in any particular congregation or parish? Of course, unless we wish churches to operate like police states, we should not expect complete uniformity. But has a sort of doctrinal relativism set in within American Protestantism (and here the Episcopal Church is Protestant) which makes the affirmations of traditional doctrine close to meaningless? It is one thing to recite the Creed as the truth; it is something apparently similar but deeply different to recite the Creed as "true for me," which generally, when analyzed, turns out to mean not true in any meaningful sense.

If communion is between really existing churches, then how the churches hold what they teach can be as important for communion as what they teach. Yet here we enter an area where it is very difficult to get accurate bearings. How do we gauge how a church, even our own, holds its teachings? Exaggerated talk of the general apostasy of the mainline churches is easy to dismiss, but there is a real problem here. In relation to the proposals before us, this problem takes at least two forms. First, there is the specific problem of the polity of the UCC and, to a significant but lesser degree, of the Episcopal Church. Second, there are general worries about doctrinal relativism. I will address both these problems in turn, and, in relation to the second, I want also to address very general worries that adopting the ecumenical proposals might mean a loss of Lutheran identity and specificity. Throughout this lecture I want to keep in mind the criterion I proposed in the last lecture: Do the problems I will be discussing stand in the way of a common life in communion consistent with the integrity of the church?

1. Polity and Authoritative Decisions

First, we cannot ignore certain questions that deal with polity and the sort of commitments the churches involved in these proposals can make. All three proposals presume that the churches involved are capable of making binding statements about what they teach and binding commitments about what they will do in the future. Different churches have different procedures for carrying out such actions. The Roman Catholic Church can authoritatively affirm the Joint Declaration only at the world level, i.e., by an action of the Vatican, while the LWF is dependent on a series of actions by its member churches. The Presbyterian Church will need not only to vote on the Formula at its General Assembly, but will need also to poll its presbyteries.

In all churches, there will need to be a process of reception, that is, a process by which the various bodies within the churches — agencies, congregations, synods, dioceses, seminaries — make these decisions their own. Reception is inevitably nonuniform. Decisions made at the national level may be taken up enthusiastically by some persons, ignored by others, actively resisted by yet others. Reception can also fail. A national resolution can remain a dead letter if it is not taken up by the faithful. This unavoidable unpredictability of reception should not, however, call into question the proposals themselves.

A more complex question has to do with the nature of the authority of the church body making the decision. The complication arises with the United Church of Christ and, to a lesser degree, but one we still must take into account, with the Episcopal Church. The polity of the UCC is not congregational in the sense that, say, the Southern Baptist Convention is congregational. Rather, the UCC describes its polity as "covenantal." The UCC defines itself as "composed of Local Churches, Associations, Conferences, and the General Synod."[1] Within the UCC structure, each Local Church, that is, each congregation, possesses an "autonomy" that is "inherent and modifiable only by its own action." One aspect of this autonomy is the authority "to formulate its own covenants and confessions of faith" (II.15). Thus, viewed constitutionally, a decision in favor of the Formula by the national General Synod of the UCC is, strictly speaking, binding only on the General Synod itself.

Nevertheless, the UCC Constitution also states that "actions by . . . the General Synod, a Conference or an Association, should be held in the highest regard by every Local Church" (II.16). John Thomas, the Assistant for Ecumenical Concerns to the President of the UCC, has argued that while the General Synod cannot make constitutionally binding decisions for every level of the UCC, the UCC has shown itself able to make genuinely "effective" ecumenical decisions, decisions made by the General Synod and then received by the local churches, conferences, and associations. The UCC has in fact entered into communion with the Disciples of Christ and with the Evangelical Church of the Union in Germany and has been an active member of the Consultation on Church Union.[2]

The Formula lays great emphasis on "the binding and effective commitment" each church would make in adopting the Formula. In adopting the Formula, the churches would "declare . . . that they are fully committed to *A Formula of Agreement*, and are capable of being, and remaining, pledged to the above-

---

1. The Constitution of the United Church of Christ, Art. II, par. 5. All further references to the UCC Constitution will be included within the text.

2. John H. Thomas, "United Church of Christ Reflections on Questions Regarding Proposed Full Communion with the Evangelical Lutheran Church in America, Presbyterian Church (USA), Reformed Church in America," unpublished paper (1996), 5-6.

described mutual affirmations in faith and doctrine, to joint decision-making, and to exercising and accepting mutual admonition and correction."[3]

This pledge does not settle every question, but it seems to me that it is very hard to ask for more from the proposals before us. The question to be decided here is not one about constitutions but about the realities of church life. If the UCC has in the recent past been capable of making and maintaining ecumenical commitments, then the question seems to me settled, even if we might wish that the process by which these commitments were made were more juridically neat. (I would note that the LWF has the same problem in an even more acute form in affirming the Joint Declaration.)

Even if one judges that the polity question is not an insuperable obstacle for the Formula, the dispersed authority within the UCC and also within the Episcopal Church raises another question. At the moment, neither the UCC nor the Episcopal Church has a binding national policy on the ordination of gay and lesbian persons living in committed, long-term relationships. Most definitely in the Episcopal Church and, as far as I can tell, also in the UCC, this decision is left to regional bodies, which decide these matters differently.[4] This variation within the churches does not directly call into question either the Formula or the Concordat. Even if one is opposed to the ordination of non-celibate gay and lesbian persons, that does not mean one rejects the validity of their ordination in the strict sense and thus this variation does not call into question the mutual recognition of ministries among the churches. In addition, the mutual interchangeability of clergy for which both proposals call (or, I think better put, mutual availability of clergy) is always said to be subject to the discipline of each church. The proposals leave the

3. Formula, p. 22.

4. For the Episcopal Church decision on this matter, see The Protestant Episcopal Church in the United States of America in the Court for the Trial of a Bishop, *James M. Stanton, Bishop of Dallas, et al., vs. The Rt. Rev. Walter C. Righter* (1996), Photocopy.

churches free to exercise their own moral discernment in accepting or not accepting the ministry of any particular person.

Nevertheless, it is one thing to say that the mutual availability of clergy is limited by such disciplinary matters as knowledge of confirmation material or ability to pass a Greek or Hebrew test. It is another when mutual availability is limited by a disagreement on important ethical questions. As I have argued from the first of these lectures, we are called to a common life in communion. This common life in communion implies a common exercise of the divinely instituted office of ministry. At what point do disagreements about the Christian life, of which ordained ministers are called to be examples, block such a common life and ministry? Hard and fast answers are difficult to come by. Disagreement about, say, the ministry of divorced and remarried persons would not appear to me to block communion. Disagreement over an issue such as racial discrimination in ordination, however, should block communion. Disagreement on the ethics of sexual orientation falls somewhere between these two, but it is difficult, at least for me, to say just where. On the one hand, if the criterion we are applying is whether a difference makes it impossible to carry out the essential activities of the church together without violation of conscience, then differences here at least border on the communion-hindering. On the other hand, the UCC and the Episcopal Church have so far lived with such differences within the much closer life of a single denomination.

I have raised these issues because I believe they point to an important aspect of the proposals before us. Voting on these proposals will be only one moment in a larger, complicated process. First, a positive vote from the various church assemblies will not have the same meaning in each case. I believe we must recognize that the UCC will need to go through a non-juridical (and thus somewhat hard to define) process of affirmation by its local and regional bodies. With all the churches, the proposals will create a structure which we will need to grow into if the new relation is to have a true life. Second, the realities created by a positive vote may not be uniform in relation to all areas of some of the churches. With the Episcopal Church and the UCC and perhaps others as well, variations that go beyond the inevitable differences in local engagement and enthusiasm may mean that communion is full and easy in some parts of the country, but strained, even in certain senses limited, in others. If we adopt the proposals, we must be ready to live with such local variations.

This inevitably unfinished aspect of the proposals before us should not, I believe, in itself block their adoption. If communion is a true common life in Christ and the Spirit, it will not spring fully grown from the mind of a national convention. It must be realized in the actual life of the church in its various aspects. This realization may not always be easy and it may not always proceed without anomalies. The question we must consider, however, is which is the greater anomaly: a lack of communion with those we cannot but recognize as churches or the variations and tensions that will come with any proposal for communion beyond the most easy and innocuous. The 1988 Lambeth Conference of Anglican Bishops described our situation well: "Throughout history Christian divisions have developed gradually and untidily. We should not expect the healing of these divisions to happen tidily or all at once."[5]

2. Relativism and Admonition

A readiness to move forward even though the way ahead has within it certain foreseeable anomalies also is relevant to the more general issue I raised earlier, the worry that adopting these proposals is at the very least an exercise in doctrinal relativism and at the worst a total surrender of any Lutheran distinctiveness over against a contentless American culture-religion. I described the question earlier as one not so much about what the churches hold but how they hold it. It makes a significant difference whether one affirms a set of religious beliefs and practices as in

5. Lambeth Conference 1988, *The Truth Shall Make You Free: The Lambeth Conference 1988: The Reports, Resolutions & Pastoral Letters from the Bishops* (London: Anglican Consultative Council, 1988), 144.

some way, however inadequately, true, or one affirms them as a useful set of heuristic devices which have a liberating or therapeutic effect. The question is not simply the reasons one has for holding certain religious beliefs and following certain religious practices, but how they are held. If they are held instrumentally, as a means to something else, rather than for reasons intrinsic to those beliefs and practices, then the nature of those beliefs and practices changes. They become moments in the pursuit of something else. American religious life, especially among the mainstream Protestant churches, certainly seems to have become increasingly instrumentalized (although one should note that one can find this trend also earlier in American religious history).[6] That for which specific beliefs and practices becomes instrumental may still be described in broadly religious ways: as spiritual fulfillment or a right relation with God. But that goal is described in ways relatively independent of the specificity of Christian belief. Piety, even spirituality, may prosper, but the faith subtly changes.

How beliefs are held makes a significant ecumenical difference. Let me contrast two ways of looking at ecumenical agreements. In an address welcoming the new relation between the Lutheran and Episcopal churches in 1982, Episcopal Bishop John Spong of Newark said that ecumenism teaches us that "the church of the future will have to learn to embrace relativity as a virtue and to dismiss certainty as a vice, . . . to accept the fact that all of us are pilgrims on a journey into the pluralism of truth, and none of us has the final answer. . . . When the Christians of the world can do this, then perhaps in that larger community of faith, worshipers and believers will include the Jews, the Muslims, the Buddhists, the Hindus."[7] Here is one ecumenical vision: No one has the final answer and so we must abandon all

6. See the fascinating piece from 1946 by H. Richard Niebuhr, "Utilitarian Christianity," in *Witness to a Generation: Significant Writings from "Christianity and Crisis" (1941-1966)*, edited by Wayne H. Cowan (Indianapolis: Bobbs-Merrill, 1966), 240-45.

7. John Shelby Spong, "Hope and Fear in Ecumenical Union," *Christian Century* (1983): 581.

claims to a truth that might exclude other religions' truth claims. Ecumenical dialogue and relations are in the end indistinguishable from interreligious dialogue and relations.

I would hope that it is clear that in these lectures I have been pursuing a different vision, one that does not flow from a general skepticism about final truth claims, but rather flows from very specific claims: that in the Christ who comes to us graciously in word and sacrament we, that is, Lutherans and many other Christians, are one. Because we are one, we should seek to live out that oneness not just in informal and ad hoc ways, but in an institutionalized, structured, ongoing common life. Such an ecumenical vision does presuppose the possibility that Lutherans have not always and everywhere gotten everything quite right. Such a vision does relativize Lutheran claims, in the sense that it insists on seeing them in relation to the wider Christian tradition which contextualizes, enriches, and sometimes corrects them. But such a vision is not an abandonment of the notion of a final truth. It rather assumes the final truth who is Christ and whose body in the world is more than just the ELCA or just the Lutheran churches and the Lutheran tradition.

The differences between these two visions of ecumenism, the church, and its teachings are difficult to grasp and settle in terms of ecumenical texts. Ecumenical dialogues have yet to find a way of addressing this issue. But what is the possible significance of this problem for the proposals before us? Let me return to the criterion I have been proposing. The question is whether a common life in communion with the churches of the Concordat and the Formula will violate the integrity of the church because communion with the mainstream of American Protestantism (and in this respect, again, the Episcopal Church is Protestant) will lead to an erosion of the classical core of Christian belief within the ELCA? Will a common life with churches, most of which have been closer to the mainstream of American Protestantism than the Lutheran churches, inevitably mean the decline of American Lutheranism into being "just another American Protestant denomination" with no theological or doctrinal substance?

Two things need here to be stressed. First, there is no reason why the proposals must or even should contribute to such a decline into relativism. The texts themselves have had the usual effect of bilateral ecumenical dialogues, namely, a renewed attention to certain basic Christian affirmations, e.g., about justification, the Eucharist, and the church. The two proposals for fellowship have both had added to them catalogues of common beliefs to make the doctrinal affirmations on which they rest even clearer. Some have been worried by the perhaps misleading language of the mutual interchangeability of clergy and the provision of the Concordat that would not require a subscription to the Lutheran confessions from Episcopal priests who might serve within the ELCA. But neither the Formula nor the Concordat need imply any change within the normal discipline of the ELCA. Recognition and mutual availability of clergy does not mean that bishops and synodical committees must give up the normal screening procedures by which they seek to control who exercises ordained ministry within the area for which they bear responsibility.

The second thing that must be said, however, is that the proposals themselves do not and cannot guarantee whether their effect will be to weaken or to strengthen the doctrinal commitments of the churches involved, including the ELCA. The crucial question here may not be whether we adopt the proposals, but what attitude we take to them if adopted. If we adopt the proposals in the belief that now there are no significant differences between Lutherans and others, that there is no future struggle in which to engage, then it is certainly possible that adopting the proposals will have a detrimental effect on life in our churches.

But I see no reason why we must take such an attitude in adopting the proposals. It is equally possible to adopt the proposals in the conviction that we are called to life in communion with those with whom we share in Christ and the Spirit through word and sacrament. Because the proposals presuppose an internally differentiated consensus, differences still exist with these churches. Because we might judge these differences not to be church-dividing does not imply that these differences are not important. Just here the model of mutual affirmation and mutual admonition offered by the Lutheran-Reformed text *A Common Calling* is helpful.[8] I certainly hope that Lutherans will have something distinctive to say and contribute in relation to the foundations of social ethics, to eucharistic and baptismal piety, to ecclesiology, and most importantly to justification by grace through faith for the sake of Jesus Christ. Adopting the proposals would mean being ready to listen and learn from others, but it need not mean retreating from fundamental Lutheran commitments. It would rather mean that we are to press commitments in a broader context.

If we adopt the proposals, we would open up a new path for Lutherans within American Christianity. The precise route of that path cannot be mapped out in advance. On the one hand, it may be that certain branches of the path turn out to be dead ends. It may be that we will discover, despite carefully developed proposals, that we cannot live a common life with certain bodies without violating what we consider to be the integrity of the church. No proposal can guarantee that such will not occur. On the other hand, new branches of the path may open up. If we adopt the proposals before us, we should then move on to consider the proposal we already have from the dialogue with the Moravians for full communion and also, I would hope, move rapidly toward a new round of discussions with the Methodists that would also, if possible, produce a proposal for communion. The process that would be begun by adopting the proposals now before us is inherently unpredictable. The proposals, especially the Concordat, call for small but not insignificant changes in how we do certain things and how we understand ourselves. In the process of realizing a common life with other churches, we should expect further change. I would hope that this change would not mean a loss of Lutheran distinctiveness, but rather a

8. Keith F. Nickle, and Timothy F. Lull, eds., *A Common Calling: The Witness of Our Reformation Churches in North America Today: The Report of the Lutheran-Reformed Committee for Theological Conversations 1988-1992* (Minneapolis: Augsburg, 1993).

shift in how we understand that distinctiveness. What should be distinctive about Lutheranism is not some possession unique to ourselves, but rather a particular perspective on what we all have been given, the one word and mission of Christ and the Spirit. The relative isolation that has typified much of American Lutheranism since the mid-nineteenth century has in some ways served us well. But what we have learned from ecumenical dialogues is that the larger context of the church and its life does not weaken that which is distinctively Lutheran, but rather provides the context in which the richness of the Reformation comes to light.

I included in the title for this lecture the phrase "the future of American Lutheranism." We need here to be realistic. Adopting or rejecting the proposals before us will not by itself decide the future of American Lutheranism. I do not believe that either adopting or rejecting the proposals will itself either save or destroy the ELCA. Yet the adoption or rejection of these proposals, and even more the perspective and attitude with which they are adopted or rejected, will make a significant difference to the shape of our future by determining the context within which certain aspects of that future are determined. Will we live out our relation with other Christians in this country within a comprehensive structure of relations of communion with a significant range of churches; will we turn in only one direction, perhaps Anglican and Catholic or perhaps Reformed and Methodist; or will we seek some form of common life that is less structured, more ad hoc, and probably more limited? At least this much is at stake in the decisions we must make this summer.

In these lectures, I hope I have shed some light on the issues we need to think about in making up our collective mind. I pray that we will make these decisions with our eyes firmly fixed on that which is prior to our decisions, on the gift we have received in Christ, who is the one head of the one body, against which neither the gates of hell nor our foolishness will ever prevail.

An Afterword:
Where Are We after the Votes?

MICHAEL ROOT

Where are we now, after the churches have voted on the three ecumenical proposals Gabriel Fackre and I addressed in our lectures? The proposals did not represent ends in themselves, however much they may represent turning points in the ecumenical lives of the churches involved. Each was a moment in a larger process. The significance of each is largely dependent on what the churches now do about the decisions they have made. The technical term here is "reception": In what way will the decisions be received by the churches, taken up into their ongoing lives in a way that makes a difference? Each decision confronts the churches with a specific set of challenges.

1. The Lutheran-Reformed Formula

The relatively ready acceptance of the Formula of Agreement between the ELCA and the three Reformed churches surprised many. As expected, little opposition arose among the Reformed, who historically have been far more open to fellowship with Lutherans than the Lutherans with them. What Reformed opposition did arise had less to do with misgivings about relations with Lutherans than with misgivings among some in the RCA about closer ties with the UCC and its degree of openness to homosexuality. The votes in the three Reformed churches were overwhelmingly in favor.

If the pattern of the past had been repeated, the Formula should have had a difficult time in the ELCA. A 1980s proposal for Lutheran-Reformed fellowship sparked intense arguments among Lutherans and failed to win acceptance among all the churches which merged in 1988 to form the ELCA. Nine months before the ELCA vote, some commentators were stating that the Formula was dead in the water.[1] In the end, eighty-one percent of the ELCA Assembly voted in favor of the Formula. What happened?

Decisions about relations with other churches tend also to be decisions about a church's own identity and so they become battlegrounds of ecclesial self-definition. In the ELCA in 1997, the Concordat became such a battleground, eliciting both more passionate support and more vehement rejection than the Formula.[2] The other proposals tended to remain in its shadow, receiving less (but perhaps more calm and rational) attention. In addition, many supporters of the Concordat believed that the passage of the Formula would increase the likelihood of the Concordat's passage, which tended to mute criticism of the Formula among some who had misgivings about it. In this way, although the tendency to see the two proposals as a package was attacked by opponents of the Concordat as a subterfuge to gain support for the Concordat, the Formula seems to have gained more from its perceived connection with the Concordat than vice versa.

One should not discount, however, a more obvious reason for the success of the Formula: it did a better job than earlier proposals of meeting the traditional Lutheran objections to fel-

1. Gracia Grindal, "Reformed and Episcopal Ecumenics: Death and Sickness Unto Death," *Dialog* 36 (1997): 5.
2. In the discussions following my lectures, the focus of questions was always the Concordat, although I was careful in the lectures to give each of the proposals approximately equal time.

lowship with Reformed churches, especially the objections that have centered around disagreements on the Lord's Supper. Some voted for the Formula with misgivings, but, when they looked at the text in detail, they found their misgivings met to the extent that a positive vote seemed more appropriate than a negative vote.[3] Church assemblies give many occasions for cynicism, but a significant number of persons voted for the Formula because they read it and were convinced.

The acceptance of the Formula now presents the churches involved with the question: so what? The European Lutheran-Reformed-United Leuenberg Agreement distinguishes between the declaration of fellowship, achieved by the acceptance of the text of the Agreement, and the realization of fellowship, achieved only in the ongoing life of the churches.[4] Action at the national level is already underway to move from declaration to realization. A Lutheran-Reformed Joint Commission is being constituted to coordinate the implementation of full communion among the churches involved. A worship service to celebrate and inaugurate the new relation is scheduled for October 1998.

Some potential stumbling blocks stand in the way of realizing the new Lutheran-Reformed communion. As I argued in my third lecture, the asymmetry in polity and ecclesiology between the UCC and the other churches of the Formula cannot be ignored, even if it did not present a reason for rejecting the Formula. What is the status of the Formula for the various conferences, associations, and congregations of the UCC? How will mutual affirmation and admonition work in localities where sharp differences among the churches exist over, e.g., trinitarian language or the ordination of homosexual persons?

Nor can the minority who opposed the Formula in the ELCA be simply ignored. If, as has been argued, this minority was made up disproportionately of pastors and if a significant number who

3. See, e.g., Faculty of Lutheran Theological Southern Seminary, "With Hope and Discretion: For a Yes to Unity in 1997," *Dialog* 36 (1997): 220.

4. See Section 4 of the *Agreement:* "The Declaration and Realization of Church Fellowship."

voted for the Formula did so with misgivings that were borne only in anticipation of the Concordat's simultaneous acceptance,[5] then some resistance to moving from declaration to realization must be anticipated.

The tendency will probably be for such resistance to be passive and silent. The Formula mandates no particular action by local or regional bodies. Some who are unenthusiastic will wait for the other to make the first move and then drag their feet a bit. If, as the debate seemed to indicate, the Formula does not stir passions even among the majority of its supporters, then passive resistance among a minority can have a deadening effect. Such passive non-reception will only be encouraged if room is not given for true mutual affirmation and admonition. Resisting Lutherans must be shown in practice that the Formula is no more a capitulation to a liberal Protestantism they find inimical than the Concordat is a capitulation to a hierarchical Catholicism its opponents wished to reject. This demonstration can only occur if continuing misgivings are both honestly confessed and honestly addressed.

One could be more sanguine about the prospects for the Formula's progress from declaration to realization if it had been more vigorously debated in the churches. Various voices, including that of the ELCA Presiding Bishop, guessed that the Formula evoked less debate than did the Concordat because the Formula asked for no changes in the internal lives of the churches while the Concordat did. The Formula thus appeared painless. The worry cannot be suppressed that proposals like the Formula (and, to a large extent, the Concordat) which aim at communion rather than merger are acceptable because they leave so much of the familiar landscape of division in place. Will the churches truly move toward a common life within the structures the Formula creates? I will return to this question at the end of this essay.

---

5. Leonard Klein guesses that as many as one-third of the clergy members of the Assembly either voted no or would have done so were it not for the Concordat. See Leonard R. Klein, "Experiential Expressivism — The ELCA's August Assembly," *Forum Letter* 26:10 (October 1997): 4.

2. The Catholic-Lutheran Joint Declaration

The only assembly voting on the Lutheran–Roman Catholic Joint Declaration on the Doctrine of Justification was the ELCA. The conclusions of the Joint Declaration, that a consensus on the basic truths of the doctrine of justification exists between the Lutheran and Catholic churches and that thus Reformation-era condemnations related to justification do not today apply, were affirmed by the Assembly virtually without dissent or plenary debate. In light of the importance of the issue under discussion, one must ask how and why this could occur.

The decision to vote on the Joint Declaration at the Assembly (rather than have the ELCA Council act on it in the spring of 1998, which also would have been constitutionally possible) did mean that the time for discussion of the text was short. In addition, many have noted that the vote on the Joint Declaration came after the shock of the narrow defeat of the Concordat, when the Assembly desperately wanted to do something positive. In this atmosphere, a vehement plenary debate would have been difficult.

Nevertheless, too much weight should not be placed on these factors. As noted in the lecture above, the Joint Declaration is not an altogether new text but intends to summarize the results of the earlier dialogues. The ELCA Council was already on record as affirming the "consensus on the gospel" of the U.S. Lutheran–Roman Catholic dialogue on *Justification by Faith*.[6] In effect, the Assembly was being asked to reaffirm a position the ELCA had already taken. Many of those calling for the defeat of the Formula and the Concordat supported the Joint Declaration.[7] One group of professors published a critique of the Joint Declaration, but it made little impact.[8] At the two hearings on the Joint Declaration

6. *Justification by Faith*, edited by H. George Anderson, T. Austin Murphy, and Joseph Burgess. Lutherans and Catholics in Dialogue, vol. 7 (Minneapolis: Augsburg, 1985).

7. See, e.g., the statements published in *Lutheran Forum* 31:2 (Summer 1997): 4-6.

8. Gerhard Forde et al., "A Call for Discussion of the 'Joint Declaration on the Doctrine of Justification'," *Dialog* 36 (1997): 224-29. One can guess that

during the Assembly, support was strong. One factor behind the lack of plenary debate over the Joint Declaration was the evident satisfaction with which most delegates read the text in front of them.

Unlike the Formula and the Concordat, the Joint Declaration is formally part of an international process. On the Catholic side, the text has been submitted for evaluation to the Vatican's Congregation for the Doctrine of the Faith. On the Lutheran side, the Lutheran World Federation is now awaiting responses from other member churches. By the beginning of 1998, additional responses have been received from the Lutheran churches in Sweden, Bavaria, Norway, Austria, and Venezuela. All these responses are positive. With one exception, the debate in churches from which responses are still to be expected points to strong support.

The one exception is Germany, where strong support has been accompanied by vigorous opposition. Much of this opposition seems to be rooted in internal problems that surround the relation between the Lutheran and United churches. While the United churches had been involved in the earlier, more general discussions with the Catholic church about doctrinal condemnations, they have not been involved in the Joint Declaration process since they are not members of the LWF. While the tone and content of the German debate is disturbing, pointing to a significant distance between German Lutheran theology and Lutheran theology in most of the rest of the world, the debate is not a clear indication that the German Lutheran churches will in the end reject the Joint Declaration. If they do so and if, as seems probable, virtually all other Lutheran churches affirm it, then serious questions will need to be asked about the theological unity of world Lutheranism.

Also unlike the Formula and the Concordat, the acceptance of the Joint Declaration will not lead directly to communion between the Lutheran and Catholic churches. As footnote nine to the Joint Declaration makes painfully clear, the Joint Declara-

this critique had little impact partially because its systematic misreading of the text was inherently implausible.

tion itself does not mean that the Roman Catholic Church would be ready to recognize the Lutheran churches as in fact churches, since it believes that certain essential features of the church (e.g., a ministry it can judge to be valid) are still missing among many if not all Lutheran bodies. If the Joint Declaration is accepted, the challenge for both groups, but especially for Catholics, is to explore what forms of fellowship short of full communion might now be possible. If Lutherans and Catholics are in agreement on what constitutes the center of the gospel, then shouldn't some greater or deeper forms of common life be realizable?

The Joint Declaration calls for further dialogue on the issues still dividing the churches (paragraph 43). Within this dialogue, what role will the achieved consensus on justification play? Here Lutherans will need to reach much greater clarity about the role they claim for the doctrine of justification. Some Lutherans have spoken as if the truth of the gospel rides on saying that the doctrine of justification is *the* criterion for the church's words and deeds rather than *a* criterion. But what does this distinction mean? Do Lutherans (or true Lutherans) in fact use no criterion other than the doctrine of justification to distinguish the true from the false, the acceptable from the unacceptable? A few moments' reflection should make clear that such is impossible. The doctrine of justification cannot decide whether the church should ordain gays and lesbians, whether the world economic order faces the churches with a *casus confessionis*, or whether baptism is the one means by which a person can enter the church. A far more careful analysis is needed of the role of the doctrine of justification as a critical tool for distinguishing the gospel from pseudo-gospels.[9]

9. For a conceptual history of talk of the doctrine of justification as a criterion, see Risto Saarinen, "Die Rechtfertigungslehre als Kriterium: Zur Begriffsgeschichte einer Ökumenischen Redewendung," *Kerygma und Dogma* 44:2 (1998).

3. The Episcopal-Lutheran Concordat

Surprisingly, the Episcopal-Lutheran Concordat ran into little resistance within the Episcopal Church. Occasional voices from the more Anglo-Catholic wing of the ECUSA raised some concerns about the text, but no significant organized or focused opposition appeared.[10] The vote in the General Convention was overwhelmingly positive.

From its first review by the ELCA Conference of Bishops in March 1991, the Concordat had been controversial in the ELCA. While the Concordat implied a significant theological movement by the Episcopal Church, it implied an organizational and symbolic shift by the ELCA; and, for all the Lutheran pride in taking theology seriously, the ELCA found this pill harder to swallow than the theological steps of the Formula and the Joint Declaration. In addition, the Concordat became a lightning rod for unresolved conflicts from the time of the formation of the ELCA. While some complained that the national offices of the church were stifling debate by favoring only supportive opinions, the opposition, well-organized and centered in one of the ELCA seminaries, engaged in what Robert Jenson called "an unprecedented and remarkably mendacious propaganda effort."[11] Ambiguous sentences in the Concordat (and there were such) were seized upon. Unfortunately, no attempt was made by this opposition to answer or engage the theological arguments (such as those made in my second lecture and elsewhere)[12] that sought to meet the concerns raised, e.g., in the Dissenting Report to the Concordat. Old criticisms were simply repeated without much attempt at real debate.

In 1995, the ELCA adopted a bylaw stipulating that any proposal to enter full communion with another church must receive the

10. For an interesting analysis of why such opposition failed to materialize, see R. R. Reno, "Desperately Seeking Communion," *Pro Ecclesia* 6 (1997): 392-96.

11. Robert W. Jenson, "The August 1997 Assembly of the ELCA," *Pro Ecclesia* 6 (1997): 390.

12. See especially the essays in R. R. Reno and Ephraim Radner, eds., *Inhabiting Unity: Theological Perspectives on the Proposed Lutheran-Episcopal Concordat* (Grand Rapids: Eerdmans, 1995).

support of two-thirds of the Churchwide Assembly to be accepted. Since the Concordat implied constitutional amendments, which would themselves have needed a two-thirds majority, the need for a two-thirds majority was already implicit. When the vote was finally taken, the Concordat received the support of 66.1 percent of the Assembly. The narrow defeat was not only a bitter disappointment for the proposal's supporters; its opponents were shocked to see that almost two-thirds of the Assembly voted for a proposal that would bring the ELCA into episcopal succession.

In the aftermath of this paper-thin defeat, a resolution was introduced calling upon the ELCA to "seek conversations with The Episcopal Church, building on the degree of consensus achieved at this assembly and addressing concerns which emerged during consideration of the *Concordat of Agreement*. The aim of these conversations is to bring to the 1999 Churchwide Assembly a revised proposal for full communion." This resolution must be carefully interpreted. First, any revised proposal is to be developed in conversation with the Episcopal Church; it is not to be unilateral. Second, it is to build on the degree of consensus achieved in the Assembly; that is, it starts from the fact that 66.1 percent of the Assembly found the Concordat acceptable as is. Third, it is to take into account concerns raised in the Assembly, without specifying which or how many concerns. Fourth, the process should lead to a revised, not a new, proposal. Fifth, this revised proposal should be ready for action by the 1999 Churchwide Assembly of the ELCA. (The ECUSA General Convention does not meet again until 2000.)

This resolution has been dismissed by some as window dressing, but it does guarantee that a process be set in place to bring something similar to the Concordat before the ELCA in 1999. At its meeting in November 1997, the Council of the ELCA set in motion a process to develop such a proposal in conversation with the Episcopal Church.[13] The process will obviously be

13. The drafting committee involved are Profs. Martin Marty, Todd Nichol, and myself for the ELCA, in conversation with Prof. J. Robert Wright, the Rev. William Norgren, and the Rt. Rev. Christopher Epting for the ECUSA.

difficult. In the amount of time available, the fundamental theological structure of the Concordat cannot be re-thought and re-negotiated. Presiding Bishop H. George Anderson has said that the revised proposal must include a sharing in the historic episcopate.[14] The primary task of revision must be to clarify both certain aspects of the proposal and the theological rationale for the ELCA entering episcopal succession as one element of fellowship with the Episcopal Church. It will then be up to the churches to decide if the proposal is acceptable.

The ecumenical importance of the decision to be made in 1999 is difficult to overestimate, both for Lutheranism and for the wider ecumenical scene. Issues of ministry and episcopacy have bedeviled recent ecumenical proposals, as the tortuous history of the Consultation on Church Union has shown. And yet, reconciliation with Rome and Constantinople is impossible without some resolution of this problem. Recent Lutheran-Anglican texts and proposals have taken a significant step forward theologically and ecclesiastically in moving beyond *esse/bene esse* debates. The continuity of the church in the apostolic mission is not a matter simply of the presence or absence of this or that element but is a complex reality. Some elements in this complex are essential in the strict sense. Others, while not strictly essential, may still become far more than optional. Because, in situations of need, some element is not strictly necessary does not imply that we are free to reject that element when need does not compel such rejection. Episcopal succession is understood as one element which, while neither being essential to apostolic continuity nor a guarantee of such continuity, is nevertheless so widely used as a living symbol of unity in the one ministry of the church in all times and places that it is at the very least desirable, if not what I describe in the second lecture as normally normative. The acceptance of such an understanding by Lutherans and Episcopalians in the U.S., reinforcing similar decisions already made in Northern Europe and proposals on the table elsewhere, would

14. Quoted in *The Lutheran* (January 1998): 48.

provide a basis of further discussions with other episcopally organized churches, most notably Rome and Constantinople.[15]

The fate of a revised Concordat is also of great significance for the future of American Lutheranism. As noted above, ecumenical decisions are also in part decisions about self-identity. A vote on a revised Concordat will be, to a degree, a vote on the kind of church the ELCA should be. Will the ELCA realize a vision of a church which is serious about the theological heritage of the Reformation and *for that reason* seeks the greatest unity possible with the theological, liturgical, and institutional heritage of the church catholic? The vote on a revised Concordat will be about more than hands and heads; it will be about how the ELCA understands its relation to the wider reality of the church.

4. The Unity We Seek

The acceptance of all three of the proposals before the churches in 1997 would have created a new ecumenical situation in America. After the failure of the Consultation on Church Union's 1971 merger proposal, church mergers across confessional lines have fallen out of favor. The COCU "covenanting proposals" that replaced the merger model have yet to be accepted. The Formula and the Concordat together would have created a network of churches in communion, committed to living out their unity in a truly common life. The network would have had its flaws; not

15. The argument that the Concordat is irrelevant to relations with Catholics and Orthodox because neither recognizes Anglican orders is doubly false. First, it ignores the importance of the theological perspective of the Concordat and similar Anglican-Lutheran texts. This perspective must be accepted by the churches if it is to be used in official discussions with others. Second, it ignores the significant difference in the Roman attitude to the orders of episcopally ordered churches, such as the Anglican churches (*Unitatis Redintegratio*, par. 13) or the Lutheran churches of Sweden and Finland (*Ut Unim Sint*, passim), and non-episcopal churches. The acceptance of the Concordat would not mean that ELCA ordained ministries would be immediately recognized by Rome, but it would put the discussion of ministry on a different and far more promising footing.

every church involved would have been in communion with every other church involved.[16] Nevertheless, it would have been a major ecumenical step forward, especially because the network of relations would have spanned the important ecumenical divide constituted by the presence or absence of an episcopacy in succession.

As it is, the actions that were taken do create a new network, even if only among churches on one side of that divide. The network in fact extends further than the churches so far mentioned, since each church is in fellowship with the other churches of its Christian World Communion and the UCC is also in communion with the Christian Church (Disciples of Christ) and the Evangelical Church of the Union in Germany. This network raises a major question for the ecumenical policy of our churches: Is this the unity we seek?

From the beginning of the ecumenical movement, the nature of the unity being sought has been a matter of debate.[17] Are we seeking organic unity, i.e., a merger that would create a single denomination? Or are we seeking only altar and pulpit fellowship? Since ecclesiology is itself one of the issues that divides the churches, it is not surprising that they do not agree on the details of the unity to be sought. Nevertheless, in recent years a consensus has been reached that the goal is *communion* or, if one likes, *full communion*. The details, sometimes important details, of what communion entails remain controversial; but such statements as that of the 1991 Assembly of the World Council of Churches on

16. A precise way of stating this is that the relations established would be symmetric (as are all relations of communion), but not totally connected. This situation can only be the case if the relations of communion established are not transitive. See Graeme Forbes, *Modern Logic* (New York: Oxford University Press, 1994), 279-81. This non-transitivity raises the question whether it is possible for two churches to have an agreement on the gospel sufficient for communion without also having an agreement on just what must be included in an agreement on the gospel sufficient for communion, since only on this basis can communion be a non-transitive relation.

17. For the history and present status of this debate, see Harding Meyer, *The Goal of the Ecumenical Movement*, translated by William G. Rusch (Grand Rapids: Eerdmans, 1998).

"The Unity of the Church as Koinonia: Gift and Calling" spell out a widely shared consensus on the fundamental nature and essential elements of communion.[18] The paragraph that seeks to list these elements (2.1) ends: "In such communion churches are bound in all aspects of their life together at all levels in confessing the one faith and engaging in worship and witness, deliberation and action."

Will the Formula and would the Concordat, however revised, establish the sort of common life this sentence describes? Both proposals fit a model of unity one might name "denominational communion."[19] The churches retain their organizational form as distinct, self-governing denominations. No movement is made toward merger. These distinct denominations, however, are to live out a common life in faith, worship, witness, and service so that one can say that, at least structurally, they are manifesting the visible unity of the church in a fundamentally adequate way. But will they? Or is the inertia of denominationalism so great that, after impressive services inaugurating the new ecumenical relation, all goes on as before? Is denominational communion the unity we seek, or is it an attempt to accept our division and rename it unity? If the Formula (and the Concordat, if accepted) does not lead to the common life described in the WCC statement, then we will need to rethink the ecumenical way forward.

This question of the ultimate ecumenical adequacy of denominational communion cannot, I believe, be answered in advance. Denominational communion is the right ecumenical model for America at the end of the twentieth century. When such communion is possible, we are called to enter it. That call, however, extends beyond votes at church conventions. It calls us

18. World Council of Churches, "The Unity of the Church as Koinonia: Gift and Calling," in *Documentary History of Faith and Order 1963-1993,* edited by Günther Gassmann. Faith and Order Paper no. 159 (Geneva: WCC Publications, 1993), 3-5.

19. I discuss the model of "denomination communion" in "A Striking Convergence in American Ecumenism," *Origins* 26 (1996): 60-64 [also published as "Communion and Unity: The Ecumenical Proposals Before Us and the Final Ecumenical Goal," *Mid-Stream* 36 (1997): 139-54].

to live out and manifest that unity in a common life as sister and brother churches, each realizing the one church of Jesus Christ in the only way possible, in communion with others. That is the task that the Formula sets before us. I hope it will be the task a revised Concordat will soon set before us, and I pray that one day such steps as that taken in the Joint Declaration will set that task before us with the Roman Catholic Church.